VAGUENESS

THE RUTGERS LECTURES IN PHILOSOPHY

Larry Temkin, series editor

Published in the series

Vagueness: A Global Approach
Kit Fine

VAGUENESS

A Global Approach

Kit Fine

OXFORD
UNIVERSITY PRESS

Oxford University Press is a department of the University of Oxford. It furthers the University's objective of excellence in research, scholarship, and education by publishing worldwide. Oxford is a registered trade mark of Oxford University Press in the UK and certain other countries.

Published in the United States of America by Oxford University Press 198 Madison Avenue, New York, NY 10016, United States of America.

Library of Congress Cataloging-in-Publication Data
Names: Fine, Kit, author.
Title: Vagueness : a global approach / Kit Fine.
Description: New York, NY, United States of America :
Oxford University Press, 2020. | Includes index. |
Identifiers: LCCN 2019051758 (print) | LCCN 2019051759 (ebook) |
ISBN 9780197514955 (hb) | ISBN 9780197514979 (epub) |
ISBN 9780197514986
Subjects: LCSH: Vagueness (Philosophy)
Classification: LCC B105.V33 F56 2020 (print) | LCC B105.V33 (ebook) |
DDC 110—dc23
LC record available at https://lccn.loc.gov/2019051758
LC ebook record available at https://lccn.loc.gov/2019051759
ISBN 978–0–19–751495–5

1 3 5 7 9 8 6 4 2

Printed by Sheridan Books, Inc., United States of America

CONTENTS

Series Editor Foreword   *vii*

Preface   *xv*

1. The Problem of Vagueness   1

2. The Possibility of Vagueness   23

3. The Phenomenon of Vagueness   45

Appendix A: The Impossibility Theorem   71
Appendix B: The Possibility Theorem   79

References   87
Index   91

SERIES EDITOR FOREWORD

In 2014, I had the distinct privilege of being chair of the Department of Philosophy at Rutgers, the State University of New Jersey. Peter Ohlin, philosophy editor at Oxford University Press USA, approached me about the idea of Rutgers organizing a major annual lecture series, for which Rutgers would carefully select among the world's leading philosophers to give a series of three original lectures that would be subsequently revised for publication in a book series by Oxford University Press. It was Peter's hope that such a series might come to be recognized as an important annual event on the philosophical calendar and might even one day come to rival the prestigious Locke Lectures, Dewey Lectures, and Tanner Lectures in stature.

I shared Peter's enthusiasm for the idea and promised to take it up with my colleagues and our administration. Unsurprisingly, the response was overwhelmingly supportive. However, it was decided that if we were going to take on such a commitment, we wanted the endeavor to involve much more than just adding another three lectures, each year to our already crowded academic calendar. We wanted to create an annual lecture series that was truly distinctive and special, one that would benefit not only our faculty but also our outstanding graduate students, undergraduates, and the wider Rutgers community. Moreover, we were especially concerned with creating a series that would be both personally and intellectually rewarding for our visiting speakers.

After many hours of discussion with my departmental colleagues and the Rutgers administration, the contours of the Rutgers Lectures in Philosophy took shape. First, the Department was committed to bringing in genuinely world-class philosophers who had already done, and were continuing to do, seminal work that was profoundly impacting their areas of research and, in some cases, the world at large. Our hope, and expectation, was that the lectures they would deliver at Rutgers, and the books based on those lectures, would help set philosophical agendas for many years to come. Bearing that goal foremost in mind, we were also committed to inviting a diverse group of speakers representing a broad spectrum of philosophical areas and interests within the analytic tradition.

Second, speakers would be asked to be available on campus for a full week and to pitch their first lecture so that interested alumni, the broader Rutgers academic community, and the general public might benefit from these internationally renowned philosophers. Their two subsequent lectures would be aimed at the high philosophical level that would most benefit the philosophy faculty, graduate students, and speaker, and would likely form the backbone of the speaker's subsequent book. Each lecture would be followed by discussion, a reception, and a dinner to facilitate serious engagement with the speaker's views.

Third, speakers would distribute drafts of their lectures, which would be read and discussed in advance by interested faculty, graduate students, and visitors. Then, there would be an intensive workshop on the distributed material during their week on campus, providing the speaker with valuable feedback and giving workshop attendees the chance to get to know the speaker and his or her views in a seminar setting.

Fourth, there would be a separate lunch meeting with the speaker for interested undergraduate majors, minors, philosophy club members, and students working on the undergraduate philosophy journal, *Arête*. As it turns out, several speakers have reported their meeting with our undergraduates to be one of the biggest highlights of their visits!

Finally, speakers would be encouraged to spend time in the department for impromptu discussions and to set up individual meetings with faculty or graduate students particularly interested in their work.

With these desiderata in mind, a little over two years after Peter Ohlin and I originally spoke, the first Rutgers Lectures in Philosophy Series took place, and now, some three years after that, the first book in the Rutgers Lectures in Philosophy series is coming out. It has been a long road, but we couldn't be more pleased by how the series (in both its lecture and book forms) has developed. It has truly been everything we envisaged it to be and more.

There are many people I would like to thank for helping to make the Rutgers Lectures in Philosophy series possible. I apologize, in advance, for the fact that nothing I say here can remotely reflect the depth of my gratitude to those who have worked tirelessly behind the scenes to make this series a success. I also apologize to anyone I inadvertently forget to mention. On both scores, please forgive me.

First, my deep gratitude to Peter Ohlin, who not only planted the seed from which this series has grown, but who has helped to nurture it and bring it to fruition at every step of the way. Peter's contributions have been both invaluable and indispensable. My thanks, also, to Peter's excellent team at OUP, from members of the Editorial Board, to copyeditors, designers, marketers, production managers, and so on, all of whom do yeoman's work in bringing a book to press and making sure that it receives the attention it deserves. Thanks, also, to Peter Momtchiloff, philosophy editor at Oxford University Press in the United Kingdom for sage advice in this project's initial stages. And a special thanks to the referees for the volumes whose conscientious comments are almost always underappreciated by everyone but the authors.

In the Philosophy Department, my biggest debt is to my colleagues, who were extremely supportive of this project from the beginning, and who have spent countless hours deliberating about the series format and possible speakers, and attending the numerous series events. I also want to thank all the graduate students who have actively participated in series events, with a special thanks to Jimmy Goodrich and Adam Gibbons, who have done much of the heavy lifting in organizing the series. I also owe a debt of gratitude to two business managers, Pauline Mitchell and Charlene Jones, our undergraduate administrative assistants, Jean Urteil and Jessica Koza, and, especially, our graduate administrative assistant, Mercedes Diaz, for all their hard work. Justin Kalef has organized the undergraduate luncheon meetings, and I am grateful to him, and all the undergraduates who have made that event one of the series highlights. Special thanks is also owed to Dean Zimmerman, current chair of the Rutgers Philosophy Department, for his crucial and unwavering support of the series.

Neither the lecture nor book series would exist were it not for the substantial support that the Philosophy Department has received over many years from the Rutgers administration, including many presidents, chancellors, vice-presidents, and deans. The Rutgers Lectures in Philosophy series thrives because of the incredibly vibrant and congenial philosophical environment that the Rutgers administration has made possible. My colleagues and I can't thank them enough. I can't possibly name every important administrator whose support has helped make the Rutgers Philosophy Department what it is today, but I need to mention a few. First and foremost, the current president of the university, Robert Barchi. President Barchi is committed to excellence and has been a great champion of our department. following the president's lead, Chancellor Richard Edwards and current Chancellor Christopher Malloy have both been enormously supportive of our department.

A number of people in the dean's office have worked very hard, and successfully, to give the Rutgers Lectures in Philosophy series a high profile not only *within* Rutgers, but *globally*. These include Kara Donaldson, who oversaw these efforts, Ian DeFalco, and John Chadwick. James Masschaele, vice dean of the School of Arts and Sciences has been supportive from its onset, as has Michelle Stephens since becoming dean of humanities. Two people are deserving of special mention: James Swenson, former dean of Humanities, and currently vice provost for Academic Affairs, and Peter March, executive dean of the School of Arts and Sciences. To each, my heartfelt thanks for all they have done over many years to support the Philosophy Department in general, and the series in particular.

Finally, my biggest thanks go to the stars of the series, the speakers whose pathbreaking work is an inspiration to all those in the field. I am most grateful to those who helped put the series on the philosophical map, by agreeing to be one of the initial five speakers: Kit Fine (2016), Sir Richard Sorabji (2017), Robert Stalnaker (2018), Jeff McMahan (2019), and Béatrice Longuenesse (2020). We look forward to seeing all these fine lectures appear in book form in the near future.

Kit Fine was everything we could have wanted in an inaugural speaker. He presented cutting edge work on a topic of fundamental importance to contemporary philosophy, he was accessible and gracious, and he was a joy to work with at every stage. The book you now have in your hand, *Vagueness: A Global Approach*, is certain to be much discussed for many years to come. I couldn't be happier, or more proud, to have it be the first book in the Rutgers Lectures in Philosophy series. Those of us associated with the series have hoped that one day it would be widely recognized as one of the most important series in all of philosophy. I have no doubt that Fine's book is a major first step toward that goal.

Again, to everyone who has helped in getting us to this point, and most especially Kit Fine, my heartfelt gratitude.

Larry S. Temkin
Series Editor
New Brunswick, New Jersey
September 2019

PREFACE

I originally presented these chapters as lectures in November of 2016 as the first of the Rutgers Lecture Series in Philosophy; and I subsequently gave a revised version of the lectures in May of 2018 as part of the Shearman Lecture Series at University College London (UCL). In this book monograph, I have presented these lectures more or less in the same form as they were given on those two occasions though I have added two formal appendices which were not part of the original lectures.

The material for the lectures has been extracted from a much longer book-length manuscript, which I hope to publish separately. I therefore hope that the reader will bear in mind that many topics that are discussed perfunctorily or not at all in this monograph will be discussed at much greater length in the book. This is a bare bones account, without the usual qualifications or consideration of objections or discussion of alternative points of view.

The first lecture (Chapter 1) was intended as an introduction to a general audience with no special expertise in the topic. It is, for this reason, very sketchy and, except for the last part, not at all original. The subsequent two lectures are more substantive. The first of these (Chapter 2) presents my general account of vagueness and the second (Chapter 3) discusses its application to three topics: the sorites argument (or paradox of the "heap"); the question of luminosity (or whether we can know our own minds); and the problem of personal identity, especially in its connection to the possibility of fission.

My ideas on the topic have developed over a long period of time. I had originally written a paper, published in 1975, defending what is now known as the supervaluational approach to vagueness but, over the years, I became increasingly dissatisfied with this approach without being able to say what should be put in its place. It gradually dawned on me that the problem with the supervaluational approach was a problem with all of the extant approaches to vagueness; they took the notion of local indeterminacy, or of a borderline case, too seriously and what was required was an approach that made the notion of global indeterminacy, or of indeterminacy over a range of cases, the central notion of interest. It was my attempt to develop this "globalist" view into a coherent and systematic position that led to the present work.

I am grateful to many people who made these lectures possible: to Larry Temkin, chair of the Rutgers department at the time, for his help in organizing the original set of lectures; to Jose Zalabardo, chair of the department at UCL at the time, who helped organize the second set of lectures; and to the two philosophical Peters at Oxford University Press, Peter Momtchiloff and Peter Ohlin, for their encouragement and support. At both sets of lectures, I had the opportunity to present my ideas to a wonderful group of faculty and students; and I am very grateful to them, as well, for questions and discussion.

Some of the material overlaps with two previous papers, "The Impossibility of Vagueness," published in *Philosophical Perspectives*, 2008, and "The Possibility of Vagueness," published in *Synthese*, 2017. I should like to thank Wiley and Springer, respectively, for granting permission to reprint from these papers.

VAGUENESS

Chapter 1

The Problem of Vagueness

The topic of vagueness has been the focus of intense philosophical debate over the last four or five decades. There have been numerous articles and books on the topic, the usual back and forth, and the usual lack of consensus at the end of it all.

But when I tell non-philosophers—or even fellow academics—that I am working on vagueness, they are often surprised. They seem to have no idea why the topic could be of any interest or significance. If you tell them that you are working on the problem of free will, of how we can be free in a deterministic universe; or the problem of skepticism, of how we can know anything about the external world on the basis of experience; or the problem of consciousness, of how there can be consciousness in what appears to be a purely physical universe, then you can expect the interest and the importance of these problems to be immediately apparent to them. But with vagueness this is not so. Vagueness, they seem to think, is something to be ignored or ameliorated but certainly not something to be studied.

Vagueness. Kit Fine, Oxford University Press (2020). © Kit Fine.
DOI: 10.1093/oso/9780197514955.001.0001

There are a number of reasons I believe the topic to be worthy of study. But before going into this, let me explain what philosophers have meant by vagueness. In ordinary parlance, the term "vague" can mean a number of different things. When your annoying guest says he intends to stay "one or more weeks" he is being vague in the sense of nonspecific. Is it one week, two weeks or, God forbid, even longer? Or when an ardent advocate of evolution says that "evolution is a fact," they are being vague in the sense of indistinct. By "evolution," do they mean evolutionary theory or evolutionary history? Or when a birther says that the place of Obama's origin is vague, he may simply mean that it is uncertain or unconfirmed.

None of these senses is the philosopher's sense. When a philosopher talks of vagueness he has in mind a certain kind of indeterminacy in the relation of something to the world. Thus the predicate "bald" is vague because it is indeterminate who exactly is bald. If you line up some men, starting with one who is completely bald, then proceed by gradual increments to one with a full head of hair, then it is to some extent indeterminate which of them is bald. Or again, the location of the summit of Mount Everest is vague since it is indeterminate where exactly it begins or ends. If I were to climb Mount Everest, then it would be indeterminate when exactly I would have reached or would have left the summit (assuming I were ever to get that far).

Thus when philosophers talk of vagueness, they are interested in the kind of indeterminacy that is characteristic of the indeterminacy in the application of such terms as "bald" or "heap" or in the boundaries of such objects as Mount Everest or a cloud. Vagueness, on the face of it, can reside in both language and the world. However, in what follows I shall mainly focus on vagueness in language, although I do hope to say something later about vagueness in the world.

Vagueness, as so understood, is largely of interest because of the issues to which it gives rise. These issues are broad and profound in their scope, but they have also turned out to be very hard to resolve. The problem of vagueness, then, is the problem of finding a satisfactory resolution to these various issues.

We may place these issues under two main heads, which I call "The Soritical Problem" and "The Semantical Problem." I do not want to suggest that these are the only issues raised by the phenomenon of vagueness and later I shall suggest some others. However, they are central to our understanding of vagueness and no account of vagueness can be considered satisfactory until it makes clear how they are to be resolved.

What I would therefore like to do in the rest of the present chapter is to say what these two issues are, to consider some of the principal ways in which philosophers have attempted to deal with them, and to explain why I consider their responses to be unsatisfactory. In the remaining two chapters, I shall then attempt to develop and defend an alternative account which I hope is free from some of the defects of the other accounts.

Let us begin with the Soritical Problem. Vagueness gives rise to paradox, to an apparent breakdown in reason, in which we appear to be able to derive a contradiction from impeccable premises by means of impeccable forms of reasoning. The most famous of these paradoxes is the paradox of the heap—the so-called sorites from the Greek for "heap." But given the male pre-occupation with cranial hairiness, it has been more common to pose the argument in terms of baldness rather than heaps. So imagine a group of men lined up before us. The first, Fred, has a completely hairless head; the last, Les, has a full head of hair; and in between is a series of men, each of whom has an imperceptibly greater amount of cranial hair than his neighbor.

Now surely Fred (the first man) is bald and Les (the last man) is not bald. It is also very plausible that if a given man in the lineup is bald then so is the man to his immediate right. For one thing, there is no perceptible difference between the two of them. Look as hard as you like, you would not be able to see any difference in the degree to which they were bald. But being bald is a matter of how someone looks; and so if the one man is bald and looks the same as the next man, then so is the next man.

For another thing, a minuscule difference in cranial coverage would not appear to make any difference to whether someone is bald. Imagine a vain man, call him "Donald," who is worried about whether he is bald. He looks in the mirror one morning and says to himself "damn, I'm bald." He is then told by his friendly doctor, Harold, that a certain product, Hair-On, will improve his cranial coverage to an imperceptible degree. Does he now have an incentive to take the product? Surely not, since a minuscule change in cranial coverage can make no difference to whether he is bald.

We now have the wherewithal to state the paradox. Fred is bald. But given that there is no relevant difference between him and the second man, the second man is bald. There is likewise no relevant difference between the second man and the third, and so the third man is bald. Continuing in this way, we arrive at the conclusion that Les is bald. But he is not bald. Just look!

What makes this a paradox is that we appear to have derived a contradiction from seemingly impeccable assumptions by means of a seemingly impeccable pattern of reasoning. The assumptions are the two "extremal" premises, that Fred is bald and that Les is not bald; and the "transitional" premises, each to the effect that if a given man in the lineup (before Les) is bald then so is the next man. The pattern of reasoning consists of successive applications of the rule of modus ponens, according to which from premises of the form "p" and "if p then q" one can validly infer a conclusion of the form "q." Thus given that Fred is bald and that if Fred is bald then the second man is bald, we can infer that the second man is bald by modus ponens; given that the second man is bald and that if the second man is bald then the third man is bald, we may infer that the third man is bald; and proceeding in this way, we may eventually draw the conclusion that Les is bald, in contradiction to evident fact that he is not bald.

We must somehow have made a mistake. Either we should not have accepted one of the premises of the sorites argument or one of the instances of modus ponens or the successive instances of modus ponens by which the contradiction was derived.

Here then is the first of our two issues. What goes wrong with the sorites argument? And given that something goes wrong, why are we so readily taken in by the argument?

We turn to the second of the two issues, the Semantical Problem. Philosophers and linguistics alike are interested in providing a semantics for natural language and for various formal languages. A semantics for a given language is a systematic account of how the expressions of the language derive their meaning. Such a semantics may take various forms but the most common form is one in which semantic values, the formal counterpart of meanings, are assigned to the meaningful expressions of the language. The simple expressions of the language are simply stipulated to have an appropriate semantic value; and rules are then given for determining the semantic value of complex expressions on the basis of the simpler expressions from which they are composed.

Many philosophers suppose that a precise language, one composed entirely of precise expressions, should be given a classical semantics. This, at its simplest, is a semantics in which the semantic value of a name is its referent, the semantic value of a predicate is its extension, i.e., the set of objects of which it is true, and the semantic value of a sentence is one of the truth-values, True or False. There are then some obvious rules for assigning semantic values to complex expressions. So, for example, a subject-predicate sentence Fa will be assigned True when the referent of the name a belongs to the extension of the predicate F and will otherwise be assigned False; and a negative sentence ¬A will be assigned True when A is assigned False and assigned False when A is assigned True.

Given a semantics for a given language, one will then be in a position to say when an inference stated in the language is valid. Thus in the case of the classical semantics, we can say that an inference from the sentences A and B to the sentence C will be valid if C takes the value True whenever A and B take the value True under any appropriate assignment of semantic values to the simple expressions of the language. To give a simple illustration, the inference from ¬¬A to A will be valid under the classical semantics since, given the rule for negation, ¬¬A can only take the value True when A takes the value True.

We now face the problem of providing a semantics for a vague language, one partly composed of vague expressions. Suppose, for example, that our language is one in which we can talk about the baldness of men of varying cranial disposition. Then what kind of semantics should we give for a sentence such as "Max is bald," where Max is someone in the middle of a sorites series for the predicate "bald," and what rule should we adopt for negation?

One might think that the answer to this question was straightforward. For why not just take over the classical semantics for a precise language and apply it to a language that is vague? Thus we can say, in particular, that a predicate, such as "bald," has a certain extension and that the sentence "Max is bald" takes the value True when Max is in the extension of the predicate "bald" and otherwise takes the value False.

However, it is a presupposition of the classical account of every sentence be either true or false, the so-called Principle of

Bivalence. It was for this reason that the negative sentence ¬A was taken to be false (or have the truth-value False) when A was not true and that a subject-predicate sentence Fa was taken to be false when the referent of a was not in the extension of F. But the Principle of Bivalence does not sit easily with the idea that the predicate "bald" is indeterminate in its application to the members of a sorites series. For how can the application of the predicate be indeterminate if it is either true or false to say of anyone of them that he is bald? And how, in this case, would a vague predicate, like "bald," differ from a precise predicate, such as "electron"?

This then is the second of our two issues. How, if at all, should the usual classical semantics for a precise language be modified so as to allow for the presence of vague terms? The two issues are connected. For, as we have seen, a semantics for a vague language should deliver an account of valid inference and, on the basis of that account, we should then be in a position to say where the soritical reasoning goes wrong. Thus a satisfactory account of vagueness should, in this way, provide a unified approach to the semantics and logic of vague language.

I would like in the remainder of the chapter to discuss three lines of solution to the two issues we have raised. I shall call them Degree-ism, Supervaluationism, and Epistemicism, though I should apologize right away for thrusting such horrible sounding isms on you. These three lines of solution are by no means the only ones that have been proposed, and my discussion of them will be somewhat superficial and far from complete. But I hope to say enough to give the reader a feel for the various positions and how they might be found wanting.[1]

The first line of solution, Degree-ism, is perhaps the simplest and most natural. A precise predicate will be true or false of any object in its range of application. We may take it to be characteristic of a vague predicate, by contrast, that its application will not in general be bivalent; there will be objects of which it is neither true nor false. The predicate "bald," for example, will presumably be neither true nor false of certain men in the middle of our lineup.

We therefore posit further truth-values "intermediate" between the extreme values of Truth and Falsehood. Under the simplest version of Degree-ism, there will be one such truth-value, the Indefinite, and so the sentences of our language will now be capable of taking three truth-values, True, False, and Indefinite, in place of the two classical values, True and False. The classical rules for determining the truth-value of complex sentences must now be extended to take account of the third truth-value. Thus under the most natural rule for negation, a negative sentence ¬A will take the value Indefinite when, and only when, A takes that value. More elaborate versions of Degree-ism may posit varying degrees of truth ranging from False, or most false, to True, or most true, through small—perhaps even

---

1. An early version of Degree-ism is Goguen [1969], and a more recent version, attempting to deal with various objections, is Smith [2008]; supervaluationism was developed in Fine [1975] and has recently been defended, in relation to the other views, by Keefe [2000]; presentations of epistemicism are to found in Sorensen [2001] and Williamson [1994]; and a useful general reader is Keefe & Smith [1997]

continuously small—increments; and, in such a case, we should provide corresponding rules for determining the degree of truth of complex sentences in terms of the degree of truth of its component sentences. Thus if degrees of truth are taken to be real numbers between 0 and 1 (with 0 corresponding to False and 1 to True), then we might take the degree of truth of the negative sentence ¬A to be 1 minus the degree of truth of A.

Even if this view provides an acceptable account of the truth-value of simple subject-predicate sentences, it is far from clear that it is able to provide a satisfactory account of the truth-value of more complex sentences. Take a patch, called Pat, on the border between red and orange and let us suppose that the sentences "Pat is red" and "Pat is orange" are both indefinite. What truth-value should we assign to the conjunctive sentence "Pat is red and Pat is orange"? Intuitively, we would like to say that the sentence is false. After all, red and orange are exclusive colors. This means that the rule for conjunction should say that the conjunction of two indefinite sentences is false. But this then has the consequence that the sentence "Pat is red and Pat is red" should also be false. Yet surely it should have the same truth-value, Indefinite, as the sentence "Pat is red."

This is the so-called problem of "penumbral connection." Pat lies on the penumbra of "red" and "orange"; it is a borderline case of both predicates. But even though Pat lies on the penumbra, there can still be logical connections between its being red and its being orange; the one can exclude the other. And it is unclear how the degree-theorist is able, within the degree-theoretic framework, to explain such connections.

I turn to the second view, Supervaluationism. Take a vague predicate, such as "bald." We suppose, as with the degree-theorist, that there may be borderline cases of the predicate, cases of which the predicate is neither true nor false. However, under the present approach, we take account of something else: the different ways in which we might acceptably make the predicates of our language completely precise. There are three important technical terms here—"precise," "completely," and "acceptably." In making the predicates of our language *more precise*, we leave the clear, or non-borderline, cases as they are and change the status of only the borderline cases, changing some or all of them from borderline cases to clear cases. In making the predicates of our language *completely* precise, we make them more precise in such a way as to leave no borderline cases—each borderline case becomes a clear case. We also insist that the way we make the predicates more precise should be *acceptable* in the sense of being in conformity with our intuitive understanding of the predicates.

Let us illustrate with our lineup. Suppose, for simplicity, that there are just two borderline cases: Max, who is the less hairy of the two, and his neighbor Ned. There are then three acceptable ways of making the application of the predicate "bald" to the men in the lineup completely precise. We can take both Max and Ned to be bald, take both not to be bald, or take Max to be bald and Ned not to be bald. There is one unacceptable way to make the predicate completely precise, with Ned, the more hairy, bald and Max, the less hairy, not bald.

Given any way of making the predicates of the language completely precise, we can provide a classical semantics for the language in the usual way. We can say, for example, that the sentence "Max is bald" is true under the first and third of the three ways above for making the predicate completely precise but false under the second of the three ways.

But this is only to assign truth to the sentences of the language relative to some particular way of making it completely precise. We now say, under the supervaluational approach, that a sentence is true simpliciter if it is true for all acceptable ways of making it completely precise and that it is false simpliciter if it is false for all acceptable ways of making it completely precise. So, for example, "Fred is bald" will be true since it is true under all acceptable ways of making the predicate completely precise, "Les is bald" will be false since it is false under all acceptable ways of making the predicate completely precise, and "Max is bald" will be neither true nor false since it is true for some of the acceptable ways of making the predicate precise and false for others.

Truth for the degree-theorist is truth from "below," since we compute the truth-value of a complex sentence from the truth-values of its component sentences. Truth for the supervaluationist, by contrast, is truth from "above," since it is only by first looking up at the different ways of making the language completely precise that we are in a position to say whether the sentence is true or false in the original unprecisified language.

One advantage of Supervaluationism over Degree-ism is that it is able to account for penumbral connection. Consider again our patch that was on the border of red and orange. We wanted the sentence "Pat is red and orange" to be false, which we could not have under the degree-theoretic approach. But note now that no way of making the predicates "red" and "orange" precise will be acceptable if it renders an object both red and orange. Thus under any acceptable way of making these predicates completely precise, the sentence "Pat is red and orange" will be false; and so the sentence will be false simpliciter, just as we wanted.

However, the approach suffers from problems of its own. Under this approach, it will be true to say that there is a last bald man, one who is preceded by men who are bald and succeeded by men who are not bald. For under any acceptable way of making the predicate "bald" completely precise, we must draw a line between the men who are bald and those who are not bald and, from among the men who are bald, there will always be one who is last. But given that there is a last bald man in the lineup, can we not legitimately ask "who is it?" And if we can legitimately ask such a question, then should it not be correct to say of some particular man that *he* is the last to be bald. But there is no such man. For whichever man we choose, there will always be some acceptable way of making some other man be the last man to be bald. Thus it looks as if, under the supervaluational approach, questions which should have answers will have no answers.

I turn to the last of the three views, Epistemicism. The two previous accounts took vagueness to require the failure of Bivalence, the principle that every sentence should be true or false, and hence called for a modification to the classical bivalent semantics. The epistemicist disputes that there is a failure of Bivalence in the case of vagueness: every sentence that expresses some content, even a vague sentence, will be true or false. He will therefore be willing to say that the sentences of a vague language have exactly the same semantics as the sentences of a precise language. Vagueness makes no difference to the semantics. By the same token, the logic appropriate to a vague language will be the same as the logic for a precise language. Vagueness makes no difference to logic.

But what then for the epistemicist is the difference between vague and precise terms? And what, in particular, is it for a predicate to be indeterminate in its application to a range of objects?

Before, under the degree-theoretic and supervaluational approaches, we took indeterminacy to be a semantic matter, a gap in truth-value or meaning. The epistemist now takes indeterminacy to be an epistemic matter, a gap in our knowledge. When a predicate indeterminately applies to some objects, it truly or falsely applies to those objects; it is just that we do not know to which objects it applies.

But the gap is not any old gap in our knowledge. I do not know how many people are in the room right now, but not because of any vagueness in the expression "number of people in the room." In this case I know what it would take for there to be a 100 people in the room, say, rather than 101. The thought is that, in the case of vagueness, we are ignorant of what it would even take for the predicate to have application in any given case; we are ignorant of the *criteria* for its application. There will indeed be a complete and precisely defined criteria for when the predicate "bald," say, does or does not apply to any given man; exactly this number of hairs of such and such a length and thickness and distribution, etc., will guarantee his baldness; exactly this number, etc., enough to guarantee non-baldness; and so on, through all the different possibilities. And yet we do not know what the criteria are.

The epistemic view has certain advantages over the gap-theoretic and supervaluational views. Like the supervaluational approach, it can account for penumbral connection. Indeed, on the epistemic view there is, strictly speaking, no penumbral connection, since there are no penumbral cases to connect. But what are commonly regarded as penumbral truths will still be true. It will be true, for example, that Pat is not both red and orange since one of the two predicates, "red" and "orange," will in fact be true of Pat and the other not.

The epistemic view, in contrast to the supervaluationist view, will not suffer from the existence of unanswerable questions. The epistemicist, like the supervaluationist, will want to say that there is a last bald man in our lineup. If now we ask, "but who is he?" then there will indeed be a correct answer: we can indeed truly say of one of the men in the lineup that he is the last to be bald. It is just that we are in no position to know that what we say is true.

Despite its merits, many philosophers (myself included) have thought this view to be unbelievable. There are meant to be some facts—presumably facts of usage—that determine an absolutely precise criterion for being bald. But how could they do this? We simply have no idea.

We can see Epistemicism as the result of a common—and what I believe is usually a misguided—philosophical tendency to identify a cause with its symptoms. We are presented with some underlying phenomenon, and because we are not sure how it should be characterized, we are tempted to identify it with the symptoms by which it is made manifest. Thus we are not sure how to characterize the mental and so we identify it with the corresponding physical behavior or we are not sure how to characterize a law and so we identify it with the regularities to which it gives rise. In the present case, we are not sure how to characterize vagueness and so we identify it with the resulting ignorance rather than attempting to get at the underlying phenomenon by which the ignorance might be explained.

Each of the views that we have considered has certain advantages and disadvantages over the others. But they also have some common failings. One of these, it seems to me, is that they are incapable of providing a satisfactory solution to the sorites paradox. Consider a degree-theoretic approach in which the degrees of truth are the real numbers between 0 and 1, with 0 being Falsity and 1 being Truth. The degree of truth of a major premise such as the conditional premise $p_k \supset p_{k+1}$ will sometimes be a little less than 1 (since the truth-value of p_{k+1} will be a little less than the truth-value of p_k). Our mistake, according to the degree-theorist consists in treating as true a statement that is not true but almost completely true.

But suppose we had used $\neg(p_k \wedge \neg p_{k+1})$ (it is not the case that the k-th man is bald and yet the (k+1)-th man is not bald) in place of $p_k \supset p_{k+1}$, as the major premise. Then when the truth-values of p_k and p_{k+1} are close to ½, the truth-value of $\neg p_{k+1}$, and hence the truth-values of $(p_k \wedge \neg p_{k+1})$ and of $\neg(p_k \wedge \neg p_{k+1})$ will also be close to ½—at least on standard ways of computing these truth-values. But we are as much, if not more, inclined to regard $\neg(p_k \wedge \neg p_{k+1})$ as true as $(p_k \supset p_{k+1})$. The degree-theorist seems unable to offer any plausible explanation of why this is so; and this suggests that their explanation of our inclination to accept the conditional premises is also mistaken.

The supervaluationists and epistemicists have what is perhaps an even more serious problem. Both take it to be true that there is a sharp cutoff, with a given man in the series bald and the man next to him not bald. But then why are we so inclined to think otherwise?

It is often supposed that we somehow confuse the statement that some man is bald while his neighbor is not with the statement that some man is determinately bald while his neighbor is determinately not bald. But why should we be inclined to reinterpret the statement in this way? One can imagine reinterpreting a statement that was false so as to be true. But why reinterpret a statement (that there is a sharp cutoff) that is true so as to be false? Nor is it that, once we take care to read the statement so as not to presuppose the presence of an implicit determinately-operator, we are somehow freed from any inclination to regard it as true.

There is another common failing, far more sweeping in its scope. But to explain what it is, I should first make a distinction that has so far only been implicit in what I have said. I have loosely talked of indeterminacy in the application of a predicate to some objects. But there are two kinds of indeterminacy that may be in question—*local* and *global*. Local indeterminacy is indeterminacy in the application of the predicate to a single object. We have a man, say, in the middle of our lineup and it is indeterminate whether or not he is bald. This notion of indeterminacy is just the same as our previous notion of a borderline case; for something to be a borderline case of a predicate is simply for the predicate to be locally indeterminate in its application to that object.

Global indeterminacy, by contrast, is indeterminacy in the application of the predicate to a *range* of cases. The term "range" is important here; we have not a single case, but a number of cases, two at the very least. Thus we may say in this sense that the predicate "bald" is indeterminate in its application to the men in our lineup. Even though the predicate may be determinate in its application to some of the men, it is not completely determinate in its application to all of the men.

The "common failing" to which I alluded concerns the relationship between global and local indeterminacy; for there appears to be no satisfactory way, under existing views of vagueness, of explaining how they relate. In arguing for this conclusion, I will need to make use of two assumptions, which I call the Compatibility Requirement and the Incompatibility Requirement.

Suppose I am presented with a sorites series for the predicate "bald" and I consider, for each of the men in the series, whether or not he is bald. I can either say "yes" or "no" or refrain from giving an answer. This is a so-called forced march.

The Compatibility Requirement states that a global claim of indeterminacy should be compatible with the minimal response in which I provide a positive answer in the first case and a negative answer in the last case while refraining from giving any answer in the other cases. There should be no coherence in my asserting both that the predicate "bald" is not completely determinate in its application to the men in the series while asserting that the first man is bald and that the last man is not bald.

The second assumption is a little harder to state. Suppose again that one is presented with a forced march but that in this case one either gives a positive answer "Yes, he is bald" or a negative answer "No, he is not bald" to each of the questions. Where there are 25 men, for example, one might respond "Yes" to the first 12 questions and "No" to the remaining 13 or perhaps "Yes" to the first 13 questions and "No" to the remaining 12. In such a case, there would surely be some kind of incompatibility or incoherence in giving these answers and yet going on to make a global claim of indeterminacy. To draw a line in this way between the men who are bald or not bald is implicitly to concede that the predicate "bald" is *not* indeterminate in its application to the men in the series.

But something more general would also appear to hold. For suppose one were to respond to a forced march by saying that each of the first nine men was not merely bald but determinately bald; that each of the next three men was borderline bald, i.e., neither determinately bald nor determinately not bald; and that each of the remaining men was not merely not bald but determinately not bald. Then presumably this would still be incompatible with a global indeterminacy claim. For a sharp line is still being drawn, not now between the men who are bald and the men who are not bald, but between the men who are *determinately* bald and the men who are *borderline* bald and, in addition, between the men who are *borderline* bald and the men who are *determinately* not bald. And the existence of sharp lines at this "higher" level would appear to be as much in conflict with a claim of indeterminacy as the existence of a sharp line at the "lower" level.

What goes for sharp lines at this higher level would appear to extend to sharp lines at higher levels still. It would not do, for example, to respond to each question within a forced march with the response that the man is determinately bald to the nth degree or that he is borderline bald to the nth degree or that he is determinately not bald to the nth degree.

The more general point is this. Consider any complete set of responses to a forced march—such as "Yes, . . . , Yes, No, . . . , No" or "Determinately Yes, ... , Determinately Yes, Borderline, . . . , Borderline, Determinately No, . . . , Determinately No." Call such a series of responses *sharp* if it draws a contrast between at least two neighboring cases. Then a claim of indeterminacy should exclude any sharp response to a forced march; it should not be possible to make the indeterminacy claim compatibly with giving a sharp response. As Sainsbury [1989] puts it, "Vague concepts are concepts without boundaries."

We can now state an Impossibility Result:

Impossibility: No putative claim of indeterminacy can meet the Compatibility and the Incompatibility Requirements.

In other words, no indeterminacy claim, whatever form it might take, can be both compatible with the minimal response to a forced march and yet incompatible with any sharp response. Vagueness would therefore appear to be impossible insofar as there is nothing that can meet the demands upon which its existence would appear to depend.

This is actually a *theorem*, susceptible of mathematical formulation and mathematical proof. I cannot provide a precise statement or proof of the theorem here.[2] But what the proof does, under the assumption of the Compatibility Requirement, is to construct a sharp response using iterations of the determinately operator. Thus the sharp response, in a particular case, might be that, for the first 20 men, it is determinately, determinately, determinately the case that they are bald, that, for the 21st man, it is neither determinately, determinately, determinately the case that he is bald nor determinately, determinately,

2. A proof of a simple version of the result is given in Appendix A and a more elaborate version is to be found in Fine [2008].

determinately the case that he is not bald, and that, for the last 19 men, it is determinately, determinately, determinately the case that they are not bald.

There are a number of ways, under existing views of vagueness, by which one might attempt to evade this result. One might claim, for example, that only incompatibility with a low level sharp response is required. However, even if there are forms of global indeterminacy that are compatible with a high-level sharp response, surely there are also forms of global indeterminacy that are not. Or again, it is a presupposition of the proof that if one is willing to assert that Fred, say, is bald, then one should also be willing to assert that it is determinately the case that Fred is bald, determinately determinately the case, and so. This too might be questioned though it is hard to see why, in the presence of a completely bald man, one should not be willing to assert that he is determinately bald to the nth degree. My own view is that none of these responses to the impossibility result will ultimately stand up; and, if this is so, then all of the existing approaches to vagueness should be abandoned and some other way of evading the result should be found.

Chapter 2

The Possibility of Vagueness

Chapter 1 stated an impossibility result. No indeterminacy claim could meet two very plausible requirements:

> The Compatibility Requirement to the effect that the claim should be compatible with the minimal response to a forced march; and
>
> The Incompatibility Requirement to the effect that the claim be incompatible with any sharp response to a forced march.

I suggested that the standard approaches to vagueness were incapable of providing a satisfactory response to this result; and here I would like to consider how a more satisfactory response to the result might proceed. This will call for a radical revision in the way that our understanding of vagueness and its logic have usually been conceived.

Vagueness. Kit Fine, Oxford University Press (2020). © Kit Fine.
DOI: 10.1093/oso/9780197514955.001.0001

The impossibility result essentially rests upon the appeal to a local notion of indeterminacy. For it is through iterations of a local determinacy operator that we able to formulate a sharp response, in contravention to the Incompatibility Requirement.

What I would now like to suggest is that the idea of local indeterminacy is a mere chimera. I hope I might be forgiven for calling it "the myth of the ungiven." We simply have no intelligible notion of local indeterminacy or of a borderline case. Even though there is global indeterminacy, there is no local indeterminacy—or, at least, no notion of local indeterminacy that is capable of being understood independently of the notion of global indeterminacy.

Most philosophers who have written on vagueness— perhaps even all—have assumed, not only that the notion of local indeterminacy, or of a borderline case, is intelligible, but that it is integral to the very notion of vagueness. Here is a sampling of quotations on the topic (I could have given many more):

Wright [2003], 93: "However borderline cases should be characterized, it is a datum that vague concepts give rise to them"

McGee & McLaughlin [1995], p. 221: "Vague predicates have potential or actual borderline cases of application."

Field [1994], p. 410: "What does it mean to say that 'bald' is vague? Presumably it means that the predicates admit borderline cases."

Williamson [1994], p. 171: "It is better to define a predicate as vague if and only if it is capable of yielding borderline cases, where the notion of borderline cases is introduced by examples."

Greenough [2003], p. 244., fn. 12: "The tradition of defining vagueness primarily in terms of borderline cases dates back to Peirce ([1902], p. 748), was continued by Black ([1937], p. 30), and receives its fullest expression in Fine [1975]= (mea maxima culpa!)."

This position has become so entrenched that it is necessary to restore ourselves to a state of pre-theoretical innocence if we are to appreciate that there is a genuine issue as to whether it should be adopted. Now I would not wish to deny that we talk in an ordinary way about borderline cases (although such talk is much less common than philosophers seem to suppose). However, it is far from clear that borderline cases in the ordinary sense of the term are borderline in the philosophical sense. A student who barely passes might be said to be a borderline pass even though, by the philosopher's lights, he would be a non-borderline case of a pass; and a case of law may be said to be borderline simply because it is hard to decide. It is not therefore clear that our ordinary judgements about borderline cases can be put to much use in sustaining the philosophical use of the notion.

But surely, it will be argued, we do not need to appeal to our ordinary judgements on the matter; we can simply *make out* the relevant notion. The most obvious way to do this is semantically, in terms of truth and falsehood: a borderline case of the predicate "bald," for example, is a case in which the predicate is neither true nor false—in line with the degree-theoretic and the supervaluational accounts (though not, I might add, with the epistemic account).

But if this proposal is to do any work, it must be supposed that there is a "strong" or gap-tolerant sense of "true" and "false" in which one can consistently claim that it is neither true nor false that Harry is bald without thereby committing oneself to the contradictory claim that Harry is not bald and Harry is bald (or not not bald). However, it may be doubted whether there really is a strong, non-deflationary, sense of "true" and "false" that could play this role. Some doubts on this score may arise on completely general grounds (as in Williamson [1994], 187–98). I myself do not find these general grounds compelling. But it seems to me that there are quite specific, and more convincing, reasons for doubting that the strong gap-tolerant notions of truth and falsity can have any meaningful application in the case of vagueness. For contrast the case in which we claim that a particular person is not bald (a "strong" denial) with the case in which we claim that it is not true that he is bald (a "weak" denial). For someone who believes in a strong concept of truth, the standards for the negative application of the predicate in the second case will somehow be weaker than those in the first case. But what is this difference? How less hairy can someone be if it is not to be true that he is bald rather than simply not bald? Can we seriously pretend to distinguish the question "is he bald?" from the question "is it true that he is bald?" so that I might be tempted to say "no" to the second question though not to the first?

These doubts extend to any attempt to explain the notion of a borderline case in terms of rules of use or conditions of application. Thus McGee and McLaughin ([1995], p. 209) have suggested that "to say that an object *a* is definitely an F means that the thoughts and practices of speakers of the language determine conditions of application for . . . F, and the facts about *a* determine that those conditions are met" and they go on to suggest that "this surely will allow for borderline cases" where a "borderline case is an object that is neither definitely F nor definitely not F" (p. 210). But the conditions of application give conditions for when a predicate is *true* or *false* of an object, and unless these notions of being true of or being false of are already being used in a strong non-deflationary sense—the intelligibility of which is the very question at issue—then the resulting notion of borderline case would be contradictory and so no borderline cases in their sense could exist.

Perhaps it will be conceded that there is no semantic route to the relevant notion of borderline case. But might there not be an epistemic route? Suppose someone is ideally situated to judge whether or not one of the men in our lineup is bald. She is completely competent in the use of the term "bald," she knows all of the relevant facts, she is rational and reflective, etc. She could even be God. We now ask her whether a given man in the lineup is bald.

One might then well think that in such ideal circumstances our subject would be capable of tracking the truth. So we have Truth Tracking:

(i)   If it is true that a given man is bald, then she is warranted in responding positively; and

(ii) If it is true that a given man is not bald, then she is warranted in responding negatively.

One might also think Warranted Suspense:

(iii) There are cases in which the subject is not warranted in responding either positively or negatively.

We can then infer that in these cases it is neither true nor false that the man is bald and hence that he is borderline.

One problem with this line of argument is that it is not altogether clear, given that our subject is capable of tracking the truth, why she is not also capable of tracking the facts. Thus instead of Truth Tracking, we would have Fact Tracking:

(i)′ If a given man is bald then the subject is warranted in responding positively; and

(ii)′ If a given man is not bald then the subject is warranted in responding negatively.

This appears to be as plausible as Truth Tracking, and for much the same reason, and yet it is in conflict with Warranted Suspense.

The reasons for accepting Warranted Suspense are also not as clear as one might think. Ideally, one would like to come up with a particular case in which the subject is not warranted in making a positive or negative response. But presumably in any putative case of this sort one should be ambivalent about whether or not the given man is bald. And it is not then clear why this ambivalence should not translate into a corresponding ambivalence over whether our subject is warranted in judging that the man is, or is not, bald.

It might be thought that, even if we are unable to come up with a particular case, there might be general grounds for thinking that a case of this sort will exist. For surely it is not true that in *every* case one is warranted in responding positively or negatively. And from this it will follow that in *some* case one is not warranted in responding positively or negatively—which is Warranted Suspense.

The issue here is subtle. If one adopts classical logic—and the Law of Excluded Middle, in particular—then the inference will indeed go through. But someone who adopts classical logic will want to say that each man in the lineup is bald or not bald, even though we are sometimes in no position to say which. But it is not then clear why she should not by the same token be willing to say that one is warranted in responding positively or negatively. For the main reason for misgiving on this score is that one sometimes appears to be in no position to say which, and this misgiving is no longer taken to have any force.

If, on the other hand, one does not adopt classical logic, then the way is open to allowing that our subject is not always warranted in responding positively or negatively without thereby being forced to admit that she is sometimes warranted in not responding positively or negatively. This, in fact, would be my own view on the matter. Truth Tracking—and even Fact Tracking—holds; and, in addition, our subject is not always warranted in responding positively or negatively. But from this, one is not entitled to infer that there actually is a case in which the subject is not warranted in responding positively or negatively; and so one is not entitled to infer, on the basis of Truth Tracking, that there exists a borderline case in which it is neither true nor false that the given man is bald or entitled to infer, on the basis of Fact Tracking, that there exists a contradictory case in which the given man is neither bald nor not bald. We thereby avoid the need to make an implausible distinction between Truth Tracking and Fact Tracking while still being able to maintain the truth of both of them.

A further line of defense remains. For surely, if a predicate is indeterminate in its application to a range of cases, then this must be because there is some kind of indeterminacy in a particular case. One or more of the cases must be to blame, even if we have difficulty in saying which they are. For how else could the indeterminacy in the application of the predicate arise?

One can perhaps agree that there must be something about the individual cases and perhaps even something special about a particular case from which the global indeterminacy arises. However, the view under consideration is not simply that but that the global indeterminacy is attributable to the *indeterminacy* in a particular case. The global indeterminacy can be localized, not merely to some underlying feature but to an instance of indeterminacy. And this may reasonably be questioned.

It may be helpful to have an alternative picture in mind. Imagine some stepping stones arranged as follows:

$$- \ - \ - \ \ \ \ \underline{\ } \ \ \ - \ - \ -$$

The stepping stones are uneven but no one stepping stone, considered on its own, is uneven; the unevenness is a global rather than a local feature of the stepping stones. Of course, there is a sense in which the middle stone "is to blame," but we can explain how it is to blame only by reference to the unevenness in the stepping stones as a whole. Considered in itself, it is not uneven. It is also true in virtue of the individual facts concerning the position of each stone, and of the middle stone in particular, that the stones are uneven. But this is not to say that the unevenness in the stones is attributable to the unevenness of any particular stone.

What I would like to suggest is that we should think of the indeterminacy in the application of a predicate in much the same way; it is, so to speak, an unevenness in the application of the predicate and that just as there is, properly speaking, no such thing as single case unevenness, so there is, properly speaking, no such thing as single case indeterminacy.

In this and Chapter 3 I shall develop this alternative point of view and show how it is able to resolve the various semantical and soritical problems that we have faced, as well as having important implications for a wide range of other philosophical problems.

A central question we face in developing a global view is how the global indeterminacy of the sort characteristic of vagueness is to be formulated. We shall consider two different formulations—one in terms of "state-descriptions" and the other in terms of the Law of Excluded Middle (LEM), a law to the effect that, for any statement P, either P or not P.

Consider again a sorites lineup of men $b_1, b_2, \ldots, b_n$, $n > 0$, going through gradual increments from b_1 = Fred to b_n = Les. With each member b_k of the series we may associate the sentence p_k = "b_k is bald"; and so corresponding to the series of men $b_1, b_2, \ldots, b_n$ will be a series of sentences $p_1, p_2, \ldots, p_n$. A *state-description in* the sentences $p_1, p_2, \ldots, p_n$ is a conjunction $\pm p_1 \wedge \pm p_2 \wedge \ldots \wedge \pm p_n$ of the sentences $\pm p_1, \pm p_2, \ldots, \pm p_n$, where each of $\pm p_k$, for k = 1, 2, \ldots, n, is either the sentence p_k or its negation $\neg p_k$. We might imagine being asked of each of the men $b_1, b_2, \ldots, b_n$ in our lineup whether or not he is bald. A state-description then corresponds to our providing a "Yes" or "No" answer in each case.

We may divide the state-descriptions in the sentences $p_0, p_1, \ldots, p_n$ into four groups:

  (I) All of the sentences $p_1, p_2, \ldots, p_n$ are accepted;

  (II) All of the sentences $p_1, p_2, \ldots, p_n$ are rejected;

  (III) Some of the sentences $p_1, p_2, \ldots, p_n$ are accepted and some rejected and at least one rejection is succeeded by an acceptance.

(IV) Some of the sentences $p_1, p_2, \ldots, p_n$ are accepted and some rejected but no rejection is succeeded by an acceptance.

There is exactly one state-description under (I), viz., $p_1 \wedge p_2 \wedge \ldots \wedge p_n$, and exactly one under (II), viz., $\neg p_1 \wedge \neg p_2 \wedge \ldots \wedge \neg p_n$. Any state-description under (III) will be of the form $\ldots \wedge \neg p_k \wedge p_{k+1} \wedge \ldots$, while any state-description under (IV) will be of the form $p_1 \wedge p_2 \wedge \ldots \wedge p_k \wedge \neg p_{k+1} \wedge \neg p_{k+2} \ldots \wedge \neg p_n$.

But what of the state-descriptions themselves? Should they be affirmed or denied? We wish to deny that the last man b_n in the series is bald. And so, given that we wish to deny p_n, we should deny the single state-description $p_1 \wedge p_2 \wedge \ldots \wedge p_n$ from the first group. We wish to affirm that the first man b_1 in the series is bald and hence to deny that he is not bald. But given that we wish to deny $\neg p_1$, we should deny the single state-description $\neg p_1 \wedge \neg p_2 \wedge \ldots \wedge \neg p_n$ from the second group. We will wish to deny that a given man b_{k+1} in the series is bald but that his predecessor b_k, who has fewer hairs on his head, is not bald. But given that we wish to deny $\neg p_k \wedge p_{k+1}$, we should deny any state-description $\ldots \wedge \neg p_k \wedge p_{k+1} \wedge \ldots$ from the third group. Finally, we will wish to deny that a given man b_k in the series is bald but that his successor b_{k+1} is not bald. For how could a minuscule difference in hair coverage make a difference as to whether or not a man is bald? But given that we wish to deny $p_k \wedge \neg p_{k+1}$, we should deny any state-description $p_1 \wedge p_2 \wedge \ldots \wedge p_k \wedge \neg p_{k+1} \wedge \neg p_{k+2} \ldots \wedge \neg p_n$ from the fourth group.

Thus we will end up denying *each* of the state-descriptions in $p_1, p_2, \ldots, p_n$; and this, I would like to suggest, is the hallmark of vagueness—or, at least, of the indeterminacy that is characteristic of vagueness. In saying that the predicate "bald" is indeterminate in its application to our lineup of men, one is saying that it is not possible to give a complete and correct description of how they are in regard to being bald, that in affirming or denying each of the sentences $p_1, p_2, \ldots, p_n$ one is bound to say something false.

There is an alternative way to express indeterminacy claims. Instead of forming state-descriptions from the sentences $p_1, p_2, \ldots, p_n$, we form the disjunctions $p_1 \vee \neg p_1, p_2 \vee \neg p_2, \ldots,$ $p_n \vee \neg p_n$, each one of which is an instance of LEM (the Law of Excluded Middle). Indeterminacy may then be expressed as the denial of their conjunction $(p_1 \vee \neg p_1) \wedge (p_2 \vee \neg p_2) \wedge \ldots \wedge$ $(p_n \vee \neg p_n)$. Thus indeterminacy, under this alternative formulation, amounts to the global falsity of LEM, i.e., to the falsity in the application of LEM to a range of cases. It can then be shown, under fairly innocuous logical assumptions, that the two definitions are equivalent.

The definition in terms of LEM allows for a further simplification. For we may define the local form of determinacy $D(p)$ of a single statement p by:

$$D(p) =_{df} p \vee \neg p$$

For p to be determinate is for p or not-p to be the case (this is, of course, determinacy *whether* not determinacy *that*). We may then define the global determinacy $D(p_1, p_2, \ldots, p_n)$ of a range of statements $p_1, p_2, \ldots, p_n$ by

$$D(p_1, p_2, \ldots, p_n) =_{df} D(p_1) \land D(p_1) \land \ldots \land D(p_n).$$

For $p_1, p_2, \ldots, p_n$ to be determinate is for each of $p_1, p_2, \ldots, p_n$ to be determinate. Finally, global indeterminacy can simply be defined as the negation of global determinacy:

$$I(p_1, p_2, \ldots, p_n) =_{df} \neg D(p_1, p_2, \ldots, p_n).$$

I should mention, in the interests of full disclosure, that these formulations are not quite correct as stated. For instead of forming the state-descriptions from the sentences $p_1, p_2, \ldots, p_n$, we should have formed them from their negations $\neg p_1, \neg p_2, \ldots, \neg p_n$ and, likewise, when forming the relevant instances of LEM. We might talk of *weak* indeterminacy when we use the unnegated sentences and of *strong* indeterminacy when we use the negated sentences. Thus the proper formulation of indeterminacy is $I^*(p_1, p_2, \ldots, p_n) = I(\neg p_1, \neg p_2, \ldots, \neg p_n)$ rather than $I(p_1, p_2, \ldots, p_n)$.

The present account of determinacy and indeterminacy has a number of interesting consequences. We should note, in the first place, that local *determinacy* will be possible on our account. Indeed, given either p or ¬p, the determinacy p ∨ ¬p of p will follow. Global indeterminacy, as we shall see, is also possible. Indeed, given a sorites series, we will be in a position to deny that the predicate has determinate application to each member of the series. But even though local determinacy and global indeterminacy are possible, local indeterminacy will be impossible. For to deny p ∨ ¬p is to commit oneself to the contradiction, ¬p ∧ ¬¬p. Thus our view is anti-localist in a very strong sense; not only is it compatible with the non-existence of local indeterminacy, but the sense in which there is global indeterminacy will be one that excludes the very possibility of local indeterminacy.

The account is able to avoid some of the puzzles that beset standard accounts of determinacy. Here is one such puzzle. It seems plausible that for any statement p, p entails determinacy whether p:

$$(1) \quad p \rightarrow Dp.$$

For how could p be the case without it being determinate whether p? What kind of possible scenario could we be envisaging here? Now determinacy whether ¬p entails determinacy whether p:

$$(2) \quad D\neg p \rightarrow Dp.$$

But from these two assumptions we can conclude that indeterminacy is impossible. For indeterminacy whether p (¬Dp) will entail ¬p by (1) and indeterminacy whether p (¬Dp) will entail indeterminacy whether ¬p (¬D¬p) by (2) and so by (1) again, in application to ¬p, it will entail ¬¬p. A contradiction.

The standard solution to this puzzle rests upon implausibly denying the first assumption, that p entails the determinacy of p. However, we can accept this assumption and even conclude that indeterminacy in the relevant sense is impossible. But this conclusion is not as troubling for us as it is for the standard theorist. For if local indeterminacy is impossible for her, then indeterminacy is impossible, period. But for us, the impossibility of local indeterminacy is compatible with the existence of global indeterminacy—which, in the present context, is all that matters.

Here is another puzzle. Let us grant, despite our previous misgivings, that p does not entail the determinacy Dp of p. We want knowledge of p, of course, to entail p:

$$(3) \quad Kp \rightarrow p$$

But we would also like knowledge of p to entail the determinacy of p:

$$(4) \quad Kp \rightarrow Dp$$

For how else can we explain how the indeterminacy of p is incompatible with knowledge of p? But one might have thought that knowledge of p should only require the truth of p, and since the truth of p does not entail its determinate truth, it remains unclear why this stronger consequence should also hold.

The standard explanation would perhaps be that for knowledge of p to be "safe," something more than the truth of p is required. Whatever the independent merits of this explanation, however, it does not appear to be what we are looking for since the reason, intuitively, that indeterminacy is a barrier to knowledge is that, in the case of indeterminacy, there is nothing to be known.

On our own view, by contrast, there is no puzzle as to why knowledge of p entails the determinacy of p, since the determinacy of p follows from p itself. We can also provide an explanation of the right sort as to why indeterminacy is incompatible with knowledge. For when there is indeterminacy in application to a range of cases, it will be impossible to know that p or to know that ¬p in each of these cases simply because we cannot be assured that p ∨ ¬p will hold in each of these cases. It is thus the absence of the relevant facts, and nothing about safety or the like, that explains our ignorance. (This issue is further discussed in the section on Luminosity in the third chapter).

The present account also bears directly on the relationship between indeterminacy and factuality. A number of philosophers have been attracted by the idea that indeterminacy consists in there being no "fact of the matter" but have had difficulty in explaining in a coherent way what this might be. Field ([2003], 457), for example, in considering the question "during which nanosecond did Jerry Falwell's life begin?," suggests that "the matter seems indeterminate, in the sense of, not a factual question." But he goes on to point out ([2003], 460) that one cannot very well deny that it is a factual matter that Falwell's life had begun by a given time N by denying:

(Falwell's life had begun by time N) $\vee$ $\neg$(Falwell's life had begun by time N)

since that would commit one to:

$\neg$(Falwell's life had begun by time N) $\wedge$ $\neg\neg$(Falwell's life had begun by time N),

which is a contradiction. He therefore embarks on the seemingly impossible task of understanding factuality in terms of determinacy in such a way as to defuse the charge that the indeterminacy of a statement has no bearing on its factuality.

But it is important to distinguish two questions here. One is the question with which Field begins, which is whether it is a factual matter when Falwell's life had begun. The other is the question he goes on to consider, which is whether, for a given time N, it is a factual matter whether Falwell's life had begun by N. In regard to the first question, there is no difficulty, on our own account, of understanding non-factuality in the naive way that Field feels compelled to reject. For we can simply deny that for each time N, Jerry Falwell's life either had begun by N or had begun by N. And this, we shall see, does not commit us to a contradiction.

In regard to the second question, we are in the same boat as Field; denial of its factuality *will* lead to contradiction. However, it is not so clear that the factuality of the specific, as opposed to the general, question is something that we should wish to deny. Indeed, the denial might appear to be self-undermining. For why should the non-factuality of Falwell's life beginning by N not be sufficient reason in itself to deny that it had begun by N?

And nor is the denial of the specific question required in order to distinguish Field's position in the way he would like from a factualist position such as Williamson's. For these purposes, the denial of the factuality of the general question should be sufficient.

The difficulty in providing an account of indeterminacy in terms of factuality has led philosophers to hold that the notion of indeterminacy is a special non-logical primitive or should itself be explained in terms of such primitives (such as "fact" or "truth" or "determination"). But if I am right, then there is no need to adopt such a view. Perhaps the notion of vagueness should be explained in terms of some special non-logical primitives, but the indeterminacy characteristic of vagueness can be explained in purely logical terms, using the usual apparatus of quantificational logic, and the idea that we should adopt some special apparatus for expressing indeterminacy simply drops out of view.

We therefore see that my position is the exact reverse of the standard views on vagueness in two fundamental respects. In the first place, it is globalist rather than localist; it takes the notion of global rather than local indeterminacy to be basic. In the second place, it is logical rather than extra-logical; it expresses vagueness—or the indeterminacy characteristic of vagueness—in logical terms and makes no appeal to any essentially indeterminacy-theoretic notions.

The present position is also at odds with the standard views in regard to the logic of vagueness. For it holds that we may consistently deny all of the state-descriptions in two or more independent sentences or the conjunction of two or more instances of the Law of the Excluded Middle. But none of the standard positions, as far as I am aware, will allow this. On the supervaluational view, for example, we cannot deny all state-descriptions since under any complete and acceptable "precisification" one of the state-descriptions will be true and it is a presupposition of the supervaluational view that there always is such a precisification. Under the epistemic view, it is evident that one of the state-descriptions is true. And under the degree-theoretic view, a gap in one of the statements will prevent us from denying *any* one of the state-descriptions.

This leaves us with a challenge. We do not wish to deny a single instance of LEM, since that would lead to contradiction; and yet we would like to be able to deny a conjunction of several such instances. We would also like our formulation of indeterminacy to get around the impossibility theorem, i.e., be compatible with a minimal response to a forced march yet incompatible with any sharp response. Can this be done?

In order to meet the challenge, I have developed a "compatibility" semantics and a compatibility logic for vague language. We might think of this semantics as obtained from Kripke's well-known semantics for intuitionistic logic (Kripke [1963]) by replacing the reflexive and transitive relation of extension on points with a reflexive and *symmetric* relation and slightly modifying the clause for the conditional.

This modeling, moreover, has intuitive significance within the context of vague language. For we might think of the points of a model as corresponding to different admissible uses of the language. The reflexive and symmetric relation will then relate two admissible uses when they are *compatible* in the sense that there is no conflict in what is true under the one use and what is true under the other. Suppose, for example, that there are 100 men in our sorites series. Then the use in which the first 30 men are taken to be bald and the last 50 men are taken to be not bald will be compatible with the use in which the first 31 men are taken to be bald and the last 49 are taken not to be bald.

A semantics for vague language may now be given by stating the conditions under which a logically complex statement will be true at a given use or "point." For simplicity, we just state the clauses for the usual sentential connectives—∧, ∨, ¬ and ⊃:

(i) B ∧ C is true at a use iff B and C are true at that use;

(ii) B ∨ C is true at a use iff B or C is true at the use;

(iii) ¬B is true at a use iff it is incompatible with any use at which B is true.

(iv) B ⊃ C is true at a use iff either (a) B and C are both true at the use or (b) C is true at any compatible use at which B is true.

Let us now put the semantics to work by showing how the global indeterminacy claims can indeed be true. Weak indeterminacy, I(p, q), will be true at any point in the model below (where the line that is drawn between two points is used to indicate the compatibility relation):

For we can see that

    (a) neither q nor ¬q is true at the point labeled p;

    (b) neither p nor ¬p is true at the point labeled q.

It follows that $(p \lor \neg p) \land (q \lor \neg q)$ is not true at the p-point by (a), nor true at the q-point by (b). So $(p \lor \neg p) \land (q \lor \neg q)$ is true at neither point; and hence $I(p, q) = \neg[(p \lor \neg p) \land (q \lor \neg q)]$ is true at both points.

We can see in a similar way that strong indeterminacy, $I^*(p, q)$ will be true at any point in the model:

We may use the semantics more generally to show how to evade the Impossibility Result. The original proof of the result will no longer go through. However, the failure of the original proof to go through does not establish that both requirements can be met. This can in fact be shown (Appendix B). For under a suitable reformulation of the two requirements, we have

    <u>Possibility Theorem</u>   The strong indeterminacy claim $I^*(p_1, p_2, \ldots, p_n))$ satisfies the Compatibility and the Incompatibility Requirements.

The conceptual and logical moves we have made are both required to evade the result. For the rejection of local indeterminacy means that we can no longer employ iterations of the determinacy operator to define a sharp response. And the adoption of our particular non-classical logic means that we can coherently formulate indeterminacy in terms of the global rejection of LEM.

It is to the great credit of the present approach that it enables us to demonstrate the possibility of vagueness! And I hope in Chapter 3 to show how the approach is also able to prove its worth in application to a wide range of more particular problems.

The Phenomenon of Vagueness

Chapter 2 developed an account of indeterminacy. It had two key features. In the first place, indeterminacy was taken to be a global rather than a local phenomenon, something that might be expressed by denying all the state descriptions in a given range of sentences or, alternatively, by denying the conjunction of the corresponding instances of LEM. Second, a semantics for a language capable of expressing such claims was given in terms of the compatibility of uses, where ¬A, for example, was taken to be true at a use if that use was incompatible with any use at which A is true.

I now wish to show how this account of indeterminacy might be brought to bear upon a number of different issues: the sorites argument; the question of whether and how we are capable of knowing our own minds; and the question of our identity in cases of fission. I hope that the range of the issues—from philosophical logic through epistemology to metaphysics—will give the reader some sense of the power of the account and

Vagueness. Kit Fine, Oxford University Press (2020). © Kit Fine.
DOI: 10.1093/oso/9780197514955.001.0001

that its ability to hold on to certain key intuitions in these other branches of philosophy will give her some sense of its overall plausibility.

THE SORITES

We begin with the sorites argument. Under a standard for-mulation of the argument, we adopt the "extremal" premises that Fred (the first man in the lineup) is bald and that Les (the last man in the lineup) is bald. For each man in the lineup, but the last, we also adopt a "Tolerance" principle (Wright [1975], 333–34):

<u>Tolerance</u> If the given man is bald then the next man is bald.

We can now derive a contradiction. For Fred is bald by the first of the extremal premises; it follows that the second man is bald by Tolerance; it follows that the third man is bald, again by Tolerance; and proceeding in this way, we may conclude after a finite number of steps that the last man, Les, is bald—in con-tradiction to the second extremal premise.

We shall find it helpful to consider another version of the argument. Instead of using the Tolerance principle to the effect that if a given man is bald then so is the next man, we use a "Cut-Off" principle to the effect that it is not the case both that the given man is bald and the next man is not bald. Thus in the first case the transitional inference has the form of modus ponens:

$$\frac{p_k \quad p_k \supset p_{k+1}}{p_{k+1}}$$

while, in the second case, it has the form of a Conjunctive Syllogism:

$$\frac{p_k \quad \neg(p_k \wedge \neg p_{k+1})}{p_{k+1}}$$

whereby we infer from a given man being bald and its not being the case that the given man is bald and his neighbor is not bald that his neighbor is bald.

From the classical point of view, there is no significant difference between the two major premises, since the material conditional $p_k \supset p_{k+1}$ is logically equivalent to the negated conjunction $\neg(p_k \wedge \neg p_{k+1})$. But, from an intuitive point of view, the two principles are very different. Tolerance tells us that the status of being bald will transfer smoothly, so to speak, from one man to the next. Cut-Off, by contrast, tells us that there will be no abrupt transition from one man being bald to the next man not being bald. Of course if there is a smooth transition then there cannot be an abrupt transition. But to deny that there will be an abrupt transition, from bald to not bald, is not to affirm that there will be a smooth transition, from bald to bald, unless we already take for granted that the next man is either bald or not bald.

The point perhaps becomes even clearer if stated explicitly in terms of truth and falsity. Tolerance permits us to make the transition from the truth of the antecedent claim that the given man is bald to the truth of the consequent claim that the next man is bald, while Cut-Off forbids us from making the transition from the truth of the antecedent claim to the falsity of the consequent claim. But to say that we are forbidden, given the truth of the antecedent claim, to assert the falsity of the consequent claim is not to say that we are thereby permitted to assert the truth of the consequent claim.

Cut-Off is an extremely plausible principle. There is something especially egregious in saying that a given man is bald but that his neighbor is not. For this would be to make a distinction when there was no relevant basis upon which it can be made. Indeed, if I am right, the truth of Cut-Off is integral to the very existence of indeterminacy, since indeterminacy requires that each state-description be false and hence that no sharp line can be drawn between the men who are bald and those who are not.

But although Cut-Off is extremely plausible, the application of Conjunctive Syllogism is not. For suppose I assert of Max and his neighbor Ned, who lie in the middle of the sorites series, that

(i) Max is bald; and
(ii) it is not the case that Max is bald and Ned is not bald.

Am I then entitled to conclude that Ned is bald? Clearly, I should not go on to assert that Ned is not bald and, given the assumption that Ned is bald or Ned is not bald, I *am* entitled to conclude that Ned is bald. But in the absence of that assumption, it is not at all clear that I am entitled to make the inference. In asserting the premises (i) and (ii), I am ruling *out* that Ned is *not* bald. But it is not clear that I am thereby ruling *in* that he *is* bald.

The invalidity of the relevant instance of Conjunctive Syllogism is confirmed by our semantics. For consider the following model:

$$p_{k+1} \circ$$
$$p_k \circ$$

It is then readily verified that p_k and $\neg(p_k \wedge \neg p_{k+1})$ are true at the base point while p_{k+1} is not.

Thus in this case, the premises of the argument are true while the rule of inference is invalid. With the conditional form of the sorites argument, the situation is the exact reverse. The rule of inference, Modus Ponens, is valid while the major premise, Tolerance, is problematic.

This gives us a solution of sorts to the sorites. But we are still left with a serious problem. For even if I am right about the invalidity of Conjunctive Syllogism and right about the relative plausibility of Cut-Off and Tolerance, still, why are we so tempted to accept Tolerance? And so why we are we still not saddled with paradox?

The answer, I believe, lies in the fact that we are tempted to make an illegitimate extension of the Cut-Off principle. Cut-Off says that we cannot go from a man being bald to his neighbor being not bald. We are now tempted to extend Cut-Off and say that we cannot go from a man being bald to its being not-true that his neighbor is bald. Now if saying that it is not-true that his neighbor is bald were just a roundabout way of saying that he is not bald, then we would have nothing new. But the intention is not simply to rule out the neighbor being bald but to rule out his having *any* alternative status. And in this case we do appear to get something new.

Moreover, under this strong or non-deflationary concept of not being true the inference from the relevant instance of Cut-Off to Tolerance would then appear to be justified. For given that it is not the case that Max, say, is bald and that Ned has some other status, then it will indeed follow that if Max is bald then Ned is also bald. Or to state the matter a little more formally, suppose we use $\bar{T}r(A)$ for "it is not-true that A" and, in our semantics, subject it to following clause:

$(\bar{T}r)$ $\bar{T}r(A)$ is true at u iff A is not true at u.

Then the inference:

$$\frac{\neg(p_k \wedge \bar{T}r(p_{k+1}))}{p_k \supset p_{k+1}}$$

will be valid. For suppose the conclusion $p_k \supset p_{k+1}$ is not true at given point u. Then p_k is true and p_{k+1} is not true at some point v compatible with u. So $\bar{T}r(p_{k+1})$ is true at v by $(\bar{T}r)$ above; and hence $(p_k \wedge \bar{T}r(p_{k+1})$ is true at v. It therefore follows that $\neg(p_k \wedge \bar{T}r(p_{k+1})$ is not true at u, as required. Thus, in this special case, Cut-Off will imply Tolerance and the paradox will reappear.

However, it seems to me that the intended extension of Cut-Off is illegitimate. This is not because it does not legitimately apply to the concept $\overline{T}r$ of non-truth. If there were such a concept, then Cut-Off would indeed be applicable to it. It is rather that there is no concept there to which the principle might apply. The broader concept of not-being-true, as opposed to not being the case, is an illusion—we can form no conception of an object having some alternative status to being F beyond its not being F; and it is because we fall prey to this illusion of there being such an alternative that we are inclined to think of Tolerance as simply following from an appropriately generalized form of Cut-Off.

The illusion is a transcendental illusion in something like the Kantian sense. It arises from thinking that we can attain an external or "transcendent" perspective on some phenomenon or practice from which no such perspective is to be had. Thus our ordinary practice in the use of vague predicates involves our forming judgments as to whether or not someone is bald or as to whether, in the ordinary sense of "true" and "false," it is true or false that the person is bald. But it is supposed, when we have difficulties in forming ordinary judgments of this sort, that we can somehow transcend our ordinary practice and arrive at a different kind of judgment, one in which the difficulties we are having can be attributed to some intermediate way in which the object might be susceptible to being bald.

This illusion, it seems to me, lies at the heart of most of the standard conceptions of vagueness. For they all accept some notion of borderline case and so they all presuppose that we can somehow attain a higher standpoint from which a judgment of being borderline F rather than of simply being F or being not F can be made. No wonder, then, that none of these attempts to solve the paradoxes of vagueness have ever been fully convincing. For far from being of any help in solving the paradoxes, acceptance of the concept of a borderline case stands in the way of—and, indeed, constitutes the principal impediment to—understanding how the paradoxes arise in the first place.

LUMINOSITY

It has often been supposed that if one is in a mental state (such as feeling cold) then one is in a position to know that one is in that mental state. But this assumption has been questioned by Williamson ([2000], 96–97). Let $t_1, t_2, \ldots, t_n$ be the series of times through which one goes by imperceptible increments from feeling freezing cold to feeling boiling hot; let c be the statement that one feels cold; for i = 1, 2, $\ldots$, n, let c_i be the statement that one feels cold at time t_i; and, finally, let $K_i p$ be used to indicate that one is in a position to know p at time t_i.

According to the "Luminosity" thesis (applied to the particular case of feeling cold), if one feels cold at t_i then one is in a position to know at t_i that one feels cold. That is, for i = 1, 2, $\ldots$, n:

$$(L) \quad c_i \supset K_i c.$$

But according to the "margin for error" thesis, if one is in a position to know that one feels cold at t_i, then one feels cold at t_{i+1}. For "at t_{i+1} one is almost equally confident that one feels cold, by the description of the case. So if one does not feel cold at t_{i+1}, then one's confidence at t_i that one feels cold is not reliably based, for one's almost equal confidence on a similar basis a millisecond later that one felt cold is mistaken" (Williamson [2000], 96–97). Thus, for $i = 1, 2, \ldots, (n-1)$:

$$(ME) \quad K_i c \supset c_{i+1}.$$

From (L) and (ME), one can derive the "Tolerance" principle, according to which if one is cold at t_i then one is cold at t_{i+1}. That is, for $i = 1, 2, \ldots, (n-1)$:

$$(T) \quad c_i \supset c_{i+1}.$$

But now given the two extremal assumptions, that one feels cold at t_1 but not at t_n:

$$(E) \quad c_1, \neg c_n$$

one can derive a contradiction in the usual way.

Given that the extremal assumptions (E) and the reasoning are not in question, the argument points to a conflict between the Luminosity thesis (L) and the Margin for Error thesis (ME). Williamson opts to retain (ME) and reject (L) while a number of other philosophers have been inclined to retain (L) and reject (ME).

However, our framework provides a middle way in which both Luminosity and something close to Margin for Error can be retained. For Margin for Error is now replaced by the thesis that it is not the case that one is in a position to know that one feels cold at t_i when one is not in fact cold at t_{i+1}:

$$(\text{T-ME}) \quad \neg[K_i c \wedge \neg c_{i+1}].$$

This is, so to speak, the "true" margin thesis and, indeed, this is the formulation most commonly employed when stating the thesis in its most intuitive form. Thus in Williamson's formulation above, "so if one does not feel cold at t_{i+1}, then one's confidence at t_i that one feels cold is not reliably based," it is the juxtaposition of being in a position to know that one feels cold at t_i and not feeling cold at t_{i+1} that is to be rejected rather than the transition from being in a position to know one is cold at t_i to feeling cold at t_{i+1}. One might therefore surmise that (ME) is not accepted on its own merits but on the basis of (T-ME).

Of course, for the classical logician, (ME) and (T-ME) are logically equivalent, and so whatever inferential role can be played by the one can equally well be played by the other. But for us, there *is* a significant difference. True Margin for Error is substantially weaker than Margin for Error; and, in the absence of the assumption that $c_{i+1} \vee \neg c_{i+1}$, which may well be questioned in the present context, one is no longer in a position to infer c_{i+1} from (T-ME) and $K_i c$, since this is an instance of Conjunctive Syllogism, which we have already seen not to be generally valid. The derivation of the contradiction is therefore blocked and, in fact, nothing stands in the way of maintaining, in conjunction with True Margin for Error, the Luminosity thesis in its positive form (L) above and also in the corresponding negative form:

$$(\text{L})^- \quad \neg c_i \supset K_i \neg c.$$

Not only *can* these various principles be maintained, but it seems to me that there are strong and compelling reasons for wanting to maintain them. The reasons for wanting to maintain Luminosity are the reasons philosophers have always had; and it is not to my purpose to consider them here. But our reasons for wanting to maintain True Margin for Error are quite different from those that have usually been given. For we wish to maintain that there is no sharp Cut-Off between feeling cold and not feeling cold. That is, for $i = 1, 2, \ldots, n - 1$:

$$(\text{CO}) \quad \neg(c_i \wedge \neg c_{i+1}).$$

This is the Cut-Off principle for feeling cold. But then given that knowledge (or knowledge in principle) entails truth:

$$(\text{KT}) \quad K_i c \vdash c_i$$

we can derive True Margin for Error:

$$(\text{T-ME}) \quad \neg[K_i c \wedge \neg c_{i+1}].$$

Thus the truth of the Margin for Error principle, under its proper formulation, can simply be seen to turn on the fact that feeling cold, like any other vague property, will lack a sharp Cut-Off and the fact that knowledge entails truth. No epistemologically "heavy weight" considerations of reliability or safety or the like need be involved; and so, from the present perspective, the attempts to argue for or against the principle on the basis of such considerations are simply misguided. In saying this, I would not, of course, wish to dispute the role that such considerations might play in other cases; it is merely that they play no significant role in the present case.

Many readers, on encountering Williamson's argument, will be inclined to think that it is soritical, that just as we should not accept the regular principle of Tolerance:

$$(\text{T}) \quad c_i \supset c_{i+1}, \ i=1, 2, \ldots, (n-1),$$

so one should not accept Margin for Error:

$$(\text{ME}) \quad K_i c \supset c_{i+1}, \ i = 1, 2, \dots, (n-1)$$

plausible as both principles may seem.

To this, Williamson will point out that there are good epistemological reasons for adopting (ME) which have nothing to do with the plausibility of adopting Tolerance. We have seen reason to doubt this line of defense. But our own line of attack is itself hardly neutral; and if it is not accepted, then we face anew the question of whether or not to put (ME) in the same soritical boat as (T).

Such issues are hard to adjudicate. But one way to proceed is to derive an unquestionably problematic tolerance principle from other principles. Given that the derived principle is soritically "infected," one of the principles from which it is derived must be the source of the infection; and so we can ask which it might plausibly be.

Consider the following Tolerance principle:

$$(\text{K-T}) \quad K_i c \supset K_{i+1} c, \ i = 1, 2, \dots, n-1.$$

If one is in a position to know that one is cold at time t_i then one also in a position to know that one is cold at t_{i+1}. I think it would be agreed that this principle is soritical in much the same way as the standard Tolerance principle $c_i \supset c_{i+1}$. But this principle can be derived from

$$(\text{K-ME}) \quad K_{i+1}(K_i c \supset c_{i+1})$$

$$(\text{TRANSFER}) \quad K_{i+1} c_{i+1} \supset K_{i+1} c$$

$$(\text{KK})^+ \quad K_i c \supset K_{i+1} K_i c.$$

For $K_i c \supset K_{i+1} K_i c$ by $(\text{KK})^+$, $K_{i+1} K_i c \supset K_{i+1} c_{i+1}$ by the application of Distribution to (K-ME), and $K_{i+1} c_{i+1} \supset K_{i+1} c$ by (TRANSFER).

In the present context, (TRANSFER) is unexceptional. We therefore face a choice between locating the source of the soritical infection either in (K-ME)—and hence, presumably, in (ME)—or in $(\text{KK})^+$. Now neither of them has the logical form of a Tolerance principle and each of them can be motivated in a non-soritical way. So in this respect there is nothing to choose between them.

However, (ME), in contrast to $(\text{KK})^+$, also appears to have a soritical rationale. For given any conditional scheme $p \supset p'$, we can think of a soritical rationale for it as resting on three considerations: first, the implication should appear to hold when there is no significant difference between antecedent and consequent; second, the implication should not appear to hold when there is a significant difference between antecedent and consequent; and third, a significant difference between antecedent and consequent can be seen to result from a series of insignificant differences. These are the ingredients, so to speak, that we need to make a soritical paradox; and they can be present even when there is no simple transfer of a property from one case to the next.

Let us use K_i^j for j iterations of K_i. Then (ME) is an instance of the following more general scheme:

$$(\text{G-ME}) \quad K_i^j c \supset c_{i+j}$$

This looks good for small j (in particular, for j = 1) but, despite what Williamson would want us to believe, it looks bad for large j. Knowledge (in principle) to the nth degree that one feels cold at t_1 does not appear to entail that one feels cold at t_n. Thus (G-ME) has all of the marks of a soritic assumption.

Contrast this now with $(KK)^+$. This plausibly rests on a standard KK-principle:

$$(\text{KK}) \quad K_i c \supset K_i K_i c$$

granted that $K_i K_i c$ implies $K_{i+1} K_i c$; and (KK), in its turn, is an instance of the following more general scheme:

$$(\text{G-KK}) \quad K_i c \supset K_i^j c.$$

This looks good—at least to many of us—for small j (and, in particular, for j = 2), but despite what Williamson would have us believe, it does not look too bad for large j. Indeed, for those of us who are willing to accept (KK), it does not look bad at all. Thus the principle in this case does not have the marks of a soritic assumption; and this suggests that the source of the soritic infection in (K-T) is (ME) rather than (KK) and that Williamson's argument is soritical after all.

PERSONAL IDENTITY

I wish finally to consider the bearing of our account of indeterminacy on cases of fission, in which an object of some kind splits into two objects of that kind and in which it is not clear what we should say about the continued identity of the original object. To take a standard example from the literature on personal identity, we might suppose that a symmetrically organized person is cut down the middle in such a way that consciousness and physical continuity within the organism is preserved within both halves. We do not then want to say that the person ceases to exist but nor do we want to say, unless we believe in souls or the like, that the person continues as one half rather than the other.

We might depict the situation as follows:

where P(rimo) is the person who exists at t before the split and L(efty) and R(ighty) are the persons who exist at t′ after the split. I have here made the common sense assumption that there is no other person who exists at the same location as Primo before the split or as Lefty and Righty after the split, although some philosophers, in dealing with the case, have wished to dispute this assumption.

Consider the statements P = L and P = R to the effect that Primo is identical to Lefty and that Primo is identical to Righty. There are four state-descriptions in these statements (where P ≠ L and P ≠ R are used to indicate the negations of P = L and P = R):

$$P \; = \; L \; \wedge \; P \; = \; R$$
$$P \; = \; L \; \wedge \; P \; \neq \; R$$
$$P \; \neq \; L \; \wedge \; P \; = \; R,$$
$$P \; \neq \; L \; \wedge \; P \; \neq \; R$$

and we are under great temptation to deny each of them. We want to deny P = L ∧ P = R, since that would mean that Primo is identical to both Lefty and to Righty and hence, by the symmetry and transitivity of identity, that Lefty and Righty are the same person; and yet, surely, Lefty and Righty are not the same person. We also want to deny P = L ∧ P ≠ R, since that would mean that Primo is identical to Lefty but not identical to Righty; and this would involve an unwarranted asymmetry between Lefty and Righty. For the same reason, we should deny P ≠ L ∧ P = R to the effect that Primo is identical to Righty but not to Lefty. Finally, we should deny P ≠ L ∧ P ≠ R, since that would mean that Primo is not identical to either Lefty or Righty and hence that he ceases to exist; and yet surely Primo does not cease to exist.

We are in familiar territory. Each of the state-descriptions in the identity statements P = L and P = R is false. We therefore have a situation in which, according to our previous account of indeterminacy, it is indeterminate which of these statements is true where this, in the present case, amounts to it being indeterminate which of the two subsequent people, Lefty and Righty, Primo is.

Within our semantics, the situation might be modeled as follows:

$$P = L \quad P = R$$

There are four points in this model: p at the bottom, p_L to the middle left, p_R to the middle right, and $p_{L,R}$ at the top. They are linked by a cycle of compatibility relations, with Primo identical to Lefty at p_L, Primo identical to Righty at p_R, Primo identical to both Lefty and Righty at $p_{L,R}$, and with no other identities holding. The points are now more plausibly taken to represent the various conceivable scenarios concerning the identities of P, L, and R rather than the various conceivable uses of the identity predicate.

It may be verified that in this model it will be indeterminate at the base point p to which of the two subsequent people Primo is identical, i.e., that I[P = L, P = R] will be true at the base point. For P = L is not true at p and nor is P $\neq$

L is true at p since P = L it is true at the compatible point p_L. P = R is not true at p_L and nor is P ≠ L true at p_L since P = R is true at the compatible point $p_{L,R}$. Similarly, neither P = R nor P ≠ R is true at p_R. This therefore establishes that $(P = L \lor P \neq L) \land (P = R \lor P \neq R)$ is not true at p, p_L or p_R and hence that I[P = L, P = R] = $\neg[(P = L \lor P \neq L) \land (P = R \lor P \neq R)]$ is true at p.

It is often thought that the case of fission is one in which we cannot preserve all of our ordinary common sense judgments. We therefore face a choice as to which of the judgments we should give up; and this has emboldened philosophers to consider all sorts of extraordinary hypotheses, such as the existence of multiple people at the same location. But it seems to me that, under the present account, we are in a position—or, at least, in a much better position—to preserve all of our ordinary judgments. For as we have seen, we can go along with our common sense judgments in rejecting each of the four descriptions of the case.

We can also coherently claim that Lefty and Righty are distinct $(L \neq R)$ and, at the same time, coherently deny that Primo ceases to exist at the later time. For what it is for Primo to continue to exist at the later time is for him to be identical to Lefty or to Righty $(P = L \lor P = R)$; what it is for Primo to cease to exist at the later time is for him not to continue to exist, which is a matter of his being distinct from Lefty or from Righty $(P \neq L \land P \neq R)$; and so what it is for Primo not to cease to exist is for it to be false that he is distinct from Lefty or from Righty

($\neg(L \neq R \wedge P \neq R)$)—which is what we wanted to say in our original description of the case.

I would now like to consider the bearing of the current analysis on three related issues: the concept of survival, the psychological criterion of personal identity, and the question of what matters.

Following Parfit [1971], it has been common in the literature on personal identity to draw a distinction between survival and identity, where a person existing at one time may survive at a later time without being identical to any person who exists at the later time. Thus, in the case of fission, it has been thought that Primo survives at the later time without being identical to either Lefty or Righty. It has also been common to think that the relation of survival must be understood, not in terms of identity, but in terms of some underlying criterion of psychological continuity or the like. Thus for a person P who exists at t to survive at a later time t' is for there to be the appropriate form of continuity (or connectedness) between P at t and some person who exists at t'.

I do not wish to deny that one may be able to provide a criterion for survival along these lines. But it seems to me that a criterion of continuity is no more required for the mere understanding of the concept of survival than it is required for the mere understanding of the concept of continued existence. For an object existing at time t to *continue to exist* at t' is simply for it to be identical to an object that exists at t' or, more simply still, it is for the object itself to exist at t'. Likewise, for an object existing at t to *survive* at t′ is for it not to be distinct from some object existing at t′ or, more simply still, it is for the object itself not to cease to exist at t′. Indeed, we might even treat the double negation of identity as a "weak" form of identity and the double negation of existence at a time as a "weak" form of existence. The form of the definition is then the same in both cases—what we require is subsequent identity or existence, but strict or unqualified in the one case and weak or doubly negated in the other.

Thus the present notion of survival is defined—or, at least, can be understood—in terms of identity: to survive is simply to be identical or to be weakly identical to some object that subsequently exists. Pace Parfit and others, it boggles the mind that survival could be independent of any relation of identity between the currently existing object and the objects that subsequently exist; and the present account is able to preserve this intimate and intuitive connection between the two notions.

Let us turn to the question of providing a psychological criterion for the identity of a person across time. Many philosophers have wanted to defend such a criterion but the possibility of fission raises enormous difficulties for their view. For under such a criterion, we would require that for any person P who exists at t and any person Q who exists at t′:

$P = Q$ iff P at t is psychologically continuous with Q at t′.

But given that identity is an equivalence relation (reflexive, symmetric and transitive) psychological continuity should also be an equivalence relation. But it would not appear to be since, in the case of fission, Primo at the original time is psychologically continuous with Lefty and with Righty at the later time even though Lefty at the later time is not psychologically continuous in the intended sense with Righty at that time.

Let us see how the psychological criterion fares when combined with the current analysis of the case. In raising this question I do not, of course, wish to be taken to be endorsing the psychological criterion (which, in fact, I do not endorse) but merely to be considering whether the difficulties it faces over fission might disappear under the current analysis.

Under our analysis of the fission case, we have distinguished two senses of identity: strict $(P = Q)$ and weak $(P \neq Q)$. Strict identity is indeed an equivalence relation, but weak identity is not. Indeed, the fission case is one in which transitivity of weak identity fails, since Primo is weakly identical (i.e., not distinct from) Lefty and weakly identical to Righty even though Lefty is not weakly identical to Righty. The objection to treating psychological continuity as a criterion of identity therefore fails when it is treated as a criterion of weak identity; and it therefore looks as if the psychological criterion of personal identity can indeed be upheld in the face of fission cases and the like, as long as it is treated as a criterion of weak rather than of strict identity.

We turn to the question of what matters. Parfit has argued that fission cases show that what matters (at the prudential level) is not identity but some form of psychological continuity or connectedness. For if what mattered were identity then the following would be true of any person P existing at t and a person Q existing at t′:

P at t cares about the well-being of Q at t′ iff P = Q

But in the fission case, Primo at t cares about the well-being of Lefty and of Righty at t′ and so Primo is identical to Lefty and to Righty by the left to right direction of the principle. By the symmetry and transitivity of identity, Lefty is identical to Righty; and so now, by the right-to-left direction of the principle, Lefty at t′ cares about the well-being of Righty at t′. But he does not; and so identity and prudential interest come apart.

But we can get round the apparent disconnect between the two notions by replacing strict identity with weak. Thus the proper formulation of the previous principle is:

P at t cares about the well-being of Q at t′ iff P $\not\approx$ Q

and the connection between what matters and identity (albeit weak identity) is preserved. Indeed, what we care about in caring about death is just what one would naturally think we care about, viz., not ceasing to exist. What we most want is not to be distinct from every person who subsequently exists but not necessarily to be identical to some person who subsequently exists (although this may be something that we further desire).

We see that, on the current analysis, we can do three things that might have appeared to be impossible in the presence of fission. We can connect survival to identity; we can hold onto the psychological criterion of identity; and we can hold onto the connection between identity and what matters. The only adjustment that needs to be made to our usual understanding of these issues is that we must use the notion of weak identity, i.e., of not being distinct, in place of the strict notion of identity. All of the claims that we were originally inclined to accept can then still be maintained.

I might mention two other interesting features of our analysis. In the first place, even though there is indeterminacy in who P is, i.e., $I[P = L, P = R]$ holds, there is no indeterminacy in who P is not, i.e., $I^*[P = L, P = R] =_{df} I[P \neq L, P \neq R]$ does not hold; and that is because the double negations, $P \neq\!\!\!/ L$ and $P \neq\!\!\!/ R$, of $P = L$ and $P = R$ both hold. Thus this is a case in which we have weak indeterminacy $(I[P = L, P = R])$ but not strong indeterminacy $(I^*[P = L, P = R])$.

In the second place, it is plausible that $\neg(P = L \wedge I[P = L, P = R])$ and $\neg((P \neq L \wedge I[P = L, P = R])$ will hold in the present case; and, as is readily verified, both of these claims will be true in the base point of the model above. This then provides a sense in which it is borderline that $P = L$ since the truth of $I[P = L, P = R]$ will prevent us from asserting or from denying

P = L (and similarly with P = R in place of P = L). However, this is not a genuine form of local indeterminacy of P = L by our lights since it is defined by reference to some other proposition (P = R). As with the stepping stones, it is only by appeal to the global form of indeterminacy, or unevenness, that the local form can be understood.

There are many other applications of the account but I hope I have done enough to provide some indication of its scope and plausibility. Essential to the success of these applications is the abandonment of classical logic. Quine many decades ago considered the possibility of revising classical logic in the case of conflict with one's other views. Although he was open in principle to such a revision he was opposed in practice. I myself would recently have adopted an equally conservative attitude. But I now believe that the existence of indeterminacy is already in conflict with classical logic and that it is only by giving up some of its basic principles that one can achieve a proper understanding of the phenomenon and even the very possibility of vagueness.

APPENDIX A

The Impossibility Theorem

We provide a formal statement and proof of the impossibility theorem. Some related results are to be found in Wright ([1987], [1992],129–33,137), Sainsbury ([1991],167–70), Graff-Fara ([2003], 196–200), Greenough ([2005], 182–83), Shapiro ([2005], 147–51), Gaifman ([2010], fn. 12), and Zardini [2011], 15–16. I shall not here attempt a detailed comparison between my result and these other results.

We presuppose an infinitary sentential language $L^\infty(D)$. The *symbols of* $L^\infty(D)$ are

(i) the sentence-letters $p_1, p_2, \ldots$

(ii) the negation operator $\neg$;

(iii) the conjunctive operator $\wedge$; and

(iv) the definitely operator D.

The *formulas of* $L^\infty(D)$ are defined according to the following rules:

    (i)   each sentence letter is a formula;

    (ii) if A is a formula, then so is ¬A;

    (iii) if Δ is a countable (i.e., either a finite or countably infinite) set of formulas, then $\wedge\Delta$ is a formula;

    (iv) if A is formula, then so is DA.

We make use the following abbreviations:

$(B \wedge C)$ for $\wedge\{B, C\}$;

IA for $\neg DA \wedge \neg D\neg A$.

$D^0 A$ for A, and $D^{n+1}A$ for $DD^n A$, $n = 0, 1, \ldots$;

$D^\infty A$ for $\wedge\{D^n A: n = 0, 1, 2, \ldots\}$;

$I^n A$ for $\neg D^n A \wedge \neg D^n \neg A$ and $I^\infty A$ for $\neg D^\infty A \wedge \neg D^\infty \neg A$.

Thus $D^\infty A$ is the formula:

$$A \wedge D^1 A \wedge D^2 A \wedge \ldots$$

Given a set Δ, we let $D\Delta$ be $\{DA: A \in \Delta\}$ and, similarly, we let $D^n \Delta$ be $\{D^n A: A \in \Delta\}$ and $D^\infty\Delta$ be $\{D^\infty A: A \in \Delta\}$. We say that the set of formulas Δ is D-*closed* if $D\Delta \in \Delta$, i.e., if $DA \in \Delta$ whenever $A \in \Delta$; and we let Δ^D be the smallest D-closed set to contain Δ. We sometimes use A^D for $\{A\}^D$, i.e., for $\{D^n A: n = 0, 1, 2, \ldots\}$. Evidently, $\Delta^D = \bigcup\{A^D: A \in \Delta\} = \{D^n A: \text{for } A \in \Delta \text{ and } n = 0, 1, 2, \ldots\}$ and $(\Delta^D)^D = \Delta^D$.

We take the formulas of language $L^\infty(D)$ to be governed by a relation of consequence $\vdash$ that holds between a countable set of formulas Δ and a single formula A (though there would be no problem in extending the relation to uncountable sets of formulas). We say $\Delta \vdash \Gamma$ if $\Delta \vdash A$ for each A in Γ and we use lists of formulas and sets to the right or left of $\vdash$ in an obvious way.

The consequence relation $\vdash$ is governed by the following three groups of rules:

(I) Structural Rules

    <u>Identity</u> $A \vdash A$;
    <u>Weakening</u> if $\Delta \vdash A$ and $\Delta \subseteq \Gamma$ then $\Gamma \vdash A$;
    <u>Cut</u> If $\Delta \vdash \Gamma$ and $\Gamma, \Theta \vdash A$ then $\Delta, \Theta \vdash A$.

(II) Rules for $\neg$ and $\wedge$

    <u>$\neg$-Introduction (Reductio)</u> if $\Delta, A \vdash B, \neg B$ then $\Delta \vdash \neg A$.
    <u>$\wedge$-Introduction</u> if $\Delta \vdash \Gamma$ then $\Delta \vdash \wedge \Gamma$
    <u>$\wedge$-Elimination</u> $\wedge \Delta \vdash A$ if $A \in \Delta$.

Rules for D

    <u>D-Elimination</u> $DA \vdash A$
    <u>D-Distribution</u> if $\Delta \vdash A$ then $D\Delta \vdash DA$.

    Note that $\Delta \vdash \Delta$ by Identity and Cut and so $\Delta \vdash \wedge \Delta$ by $\wedge$-Introduction. Use of the structural rules will often be implicit.

    We define *definite consequence* or *commitment* by:

$$\Delta \vdash^{D} A \text{ if } \Delta^{D} \vdash A^{D}.$$

In fact, definite consequence only requires strengthening on the left:

<u>Lemma 1</u>   If $\Delta \vdash^{D} A$ iff $\Delta^{D} \vdash A$

<u>Proof</u>   The left-to-right direction is trivial. For the right-to-left direction, assume $\Delta^{D} \vdash A$. By D-Distribution, $D(\Delta^{D}) \vdash DA$. But $D(\Delta^{D}) \subseteq \Delta^{D}$. So by Weakening, $\Delta^{D} \vdash DA$. Iterating the argument, $\Delta^{D} \vdash D^{n}A$ for $n = 2, 3, \ldots$ But then $\Delta^{D} \vdash D^{n}A$ for $n = 0, 1, 2, \ldots$; and so $\Delta^{D} \vdash D^{\infty}A$ by $\wedge$-Introduction.

<u>Lemma 2</u> $\vdash^D$ conforms to the structural rules of Identity, Weakening, and Cut.

<u>Proof</u> We consider each rule in turn.

<u>Identity</u> $A^D \vdash A$ by Identity and Weakening for $\vdash$; and so $A \vdash^D A$, by lemma 1.

<u>Weakening</u> Suppose $\Delta \vdash^D A$ and $\Delta \subseteq \Gamma$. Then $\Delta^D \subseteq \Gamma^D$. So by Weakening for $\vdash$, $\Gamma^D \vdash A$; and hence $\Gamma \vdash^D A$ (again by lemma 1).

<u>Cut</u> Suppose $\Delta \vdash^D \Gamma$ and $\Gamma, \Theta \vdash^D A$. Then $\Delta^D \vdash \Gamma^D$ and $\Gamma^D, \Theta^D \vdash A^D$. By Cut for $\vdash$, $\Delta^D, \Theta^D \vdash A^D$; and consequently, $\Delta, \Theta \vdash^D A$.

Definite consequence conforms to the rule of D-Introduction, i.e. that $A \vdash^D DA$, since $A^D \vdash DA$ by Identity and Weakening.

Reductio holds in the following modified form for definite consequence:

<u>Lemma 3</u> If $\Delta, A \vdash^D B, \neg B$ then $\Delta \vdash^D \neg D^\infty A$

<u>Proof</u> Suppose $\Delta, A \vdash^D B, \neg B$. Then $\Delta^D, A^D \vdash B, \neg B$. By $\wedge$-Elimination, $D^\infty A \vdash A^D$ and so, by Cut, $\Delta^D, D^\infty A \vdash B, \neg B$. But then by reductio for $\vdash$, $\Delta^D \vdash \neg D^\infty A$; and consequently, $\Delta \vdash^D \neg D^\infty A$.

To state the impossibility result, we need some further terminology. A set of formulas Δ is said to be *inconsistent* if, for some formula B, $\Delta \vdash B$ and $\Delta \vdash \neg B$ and Δ is otherwise said to be *consistent*. Likewise, Δ is said to be *incompatible* if, for some formula B, $\Delta \vdash^D B$ and $\Delta \vdash^D \neg B$ and Δ is otherwise said to be *compatible*. Δ is said to be *inconsistent* (or *incompatible*) *with* the set Γ if $\Delta \cup \Gamma$ is inconsistent (or incompatible).

Let p be an any sentence-letter, fixed for the purposes of the following discussion. Then an *individual response* is a formula $A(p)$ whose sole sentence-letter is p; and the formula A is a *response to* the question of B if it is of the form $A(B)$, where $A(p)$ is an individual response. A *collective response* is a sequence $A_1(p)$, $A_2(p), \ldots, A_n(p)$ of individual responses; and $A_1, A_2, \ldots, A_n$ is said to be a *collective response to* $B_1, B_2, \ldots, B_n$ if $A_1, A_2, \ldots, A_n$ are respectively of the form $A_1(B_1)$, $A_2(B_2), \ldots, A_n(B_n)$, where $A_1(p), A_2(p), \ldots, A_n(p)$ is a collective response.

We say that the collective response $A_1, A_2, \ldots, A_n$ is *sharp* if

(i) $A_i \neq A_j$ for some i, j $\leq$ n;

(ii) A_i is inconsistent with A_j or $A_i = A_j$ for $1 \leq i < j \leq n$.

In a sharp response, we give any two questions the same answer or inconsistent answers, with at least two of the answers not being the same (and similarly in regard to a sharp response *to* $B_1, B_2, \ldots, B_n$).

Call $\{B_0, \neg B_{n+1}\}$ the *extremal response* to the formulas $B_0, B_1, \ldots, B_{n+1}$, $n \geq 0$, With this terminology in place, we are now in a position to state and prove the result:

<u>Theorem 1</u>   Take any formulas $B_0, B_1, \ldots, B_{n+1}$, $n \geq 0$. Then there is no set of formulas Δ_0 which is compatible with the extremal response and yet incompatible with any sharp response to $B_0, B_1, \ldots, B_{n+1}$.

<u>Proof</u>   The proof is somewhat reminiscent of the proof of Lindenbaum's Lemma. Take any formulas $B_0, B_1, \ldots, B_{n+1}$ and any set of formulas Δ_0 compatible with B_0 and $\neg B_{n+1}$. We show that Δ_0 is compatible with a sharp response to $B_0, B_1, \ldots, B_{n+1}$.

To this end, we "blow up" Δ_0 to a set Δ_{n+1} from which a compatible sharp response can be more readily discerned. We let $\Delta_1 = \Delta_0 \cup \{B_0, \neg B_{n+1}\}$ and, for $k = 1, 2, \ldots, n$, we let:

$$\Delta_{k+1} = \Delta_k \cup \{B_k\} \text{ if } \Delta_k \text{ is compatible with } B_k,$$
$$= \Delta_k \cup \{\neg B_k\} \text{ if } \Delta_k \text{ is compatible with } \neg B_k$$
$$= \Delta_{k-1} \text{ otherwise.}$$

It is evident from the construction that

(1) Δ_k is compatible for $k = 0, 1, \ldots, n + 1$, and

(2) $\Delta_k \subseteq \Delta_l$ for $0 \leq k < l \leq n + 1$.

Using Δ_{n+1}, we define a collective response $A_0(p), A_1(p), \ldots, A_{n+1}(p)$ (and a corresponding collective response $A_0(B_1), A_1(B_2), \ldots, A_{n+1}(B_{n+1})$ to $B_0, B_1, \ldots, B_{n+1}$). Where $k = 0, 1, \ldots, n + 1$:

(a) $A_k(p) = D^\infty(p)$ if $B_k \in \Delta_n$,
(b) $A_k(p) = D^\infty(\neg p)$ if $\neg B_k \in \Delta_n$, and
(c) $A_k(p) = I^\infty(p)$ otherwise.

The collective response is well-defined since if $B_k \in \Delta_{n+1}$ and $\neg B_k \in \Delta_{n+1}$ for some $k = 0, 1, \ldots, n + 1$, Δ_{n+1} would not be compatible by Weakening and Cut for $\vdash^D$, which runs contrary to (1) above.

We may now show:

(3) $\Delta_{n+1} \vdash^D A_k(B_k)$ for $k = 0, 1, \ldots, n + 1$.

<u>Pf.</u> There are three cases:

$B_k \in \Delta_{n+1}$. In this case, $A_k(B_k)$ is the formula $D^\infty(B_k)$. But $B_k \vdash^D B_k{}^D$ and $B_k{}^D \vdash^D \wedge(B_k{}^D) = D^\infty(B_k)$ by $\wedge$-Introduction. So by the structural rules for $\vdash^D$, $\Delta_{n+1} \vdash D^\infty(B_k)$.

$\neg B_k \in \Delta_{n+1}$. Similar to the previous case but with $\neg B_k$ in place of B_k.

$B_k, \neg B_k \notin \Delta_{n+1}$. In this case, $A_k(B_k)$ is the formula $I^\infty(B_k)$. Since $B_k, \neg B_k \notin \Delta_n$, it is clear from the construction that neither B_k nor $\neg B_k$ is compatible with Δ_k and hence, by (2), neither is compatible with Δ_n. So $\Delta_k, B_k \vdash^D C, \neg C$ for some formula C and $\Delta_k, \neg B_k \vdash^D C', \neg C'$ for some formula C'. By Reductio for $\vdash^D$, $\Delta_k \vdash^D \neg D^\infty(B_k)$ and $\Delta_k \vdash^D \neg D^\infty(\neg B_k)$; so by $\wedge$-Introduction, $\Delta_k \vdash^D I^\infty(B_k)$; and so by Weakening, $\Delta_n \vdash^D I^\infty(B_k)$.

Since Δ_{n+1} is compatible by (1) and $\Delta_{n+1} \vdash^D A_k(B_k)$ for $k = 0, 1, \ldots, n+1$ by (3), it follows that Δ_{n+1} is compatible with the response $A_0(B_0), A_1(B_1), \ldots, A_{n+1}(B_{n+1})$ to $B_0, B_1, \ldots, B_{n+1}$ and hence so is the subset Δ_0 of Δ_{n+1}. It remains to show that the response $A_0(p), A_1(p), \ldots, A_{n+1}(p)$ is sharp. Since $B_1 \in \Delta_1$, $A_1(p) = D^\infty(p)$; and since $\neg B_{n+1} \in \Delta_1$, $A_{n+1}(p) = D^\infty(\neg p)$. This establishes the first condition for being a sharp response, viz., that two of the individual responses should not be the same. Now the responses $A_0(p)$, $A_1(p)$, . . . , $A_{n+1}(p)$ are of one of the three following forms: $D^\infty(p)$, $D^\infty(\neg p)$, and $I^\infty(p)$. The first two are truth-functionally inconsistent with the third (since $I^\infty(p)$ is the formula $\neg D^\infty p \wedge \neg D^\infty \neg p$) and the first two formulas are inconsistent with one another (since $D^\infty(p) \vdash p$ and $D^\infty(\neg p) \vdash \neg p$). This establishes the second condition for being a sharp response and we are done.

The collective response yielded by the proof of theorem contains three distinct individual responses—$D^\infty(p)$, $D^\infty(\neg p)$, and $I^\infty(p)$. But we may readily obtain a collective response that contains only two distinct individual responses by replacing the responses $D^\infty(p)$ or $D^\infty(\neg p)$, wherever they occur, with $\neg I^\infty(p)$. Call a response $A_0(p)$, $A_1(p)$, . . . , $A_{n+1}(p)$ *bipartite* if there are exactly two formulas in the set $\{A_0(p), A_1(p), . . . , A_{n+1}(p)\}$. We then have

<u>Corollary</u>   Take any formulas B_0, B_1, . . . , B_{n+1}, $n \geq 0$. Then there is no set of formulas Δ_0 compatible with the extremal response and yet incompatible with any sharp bipartite response to B_1, B_2, . . . , B_{n+1}.

APPENDIX B

The Possibility Theorem

We state the semantics for the propositional version of compatibilist logic (**CL**) and establish the possibility theorem. A related semantics, for quantum logic, is to be found in Goldblatt [1974].

The Compatibilist Semantics

We take a *model **M*** of **CL** to be a triple $(U, ||, \varphi)$, where

C(i) U (points or uses) is a non-empty set;

C(ii) $||$ (compatibility) is a reflexive and symmetric relation on U;

C(iii) φ (valuation) is a function from SL into $\wp(U)$.

Relative to a model ***M***, *truth* of a formula A *at* a point u ($u \vDash A$) is defined by the following clauses:

TC(i) $u \vDash p$ iff $u \in \varphi(p)$

TC(ii) never $u \vDash \perp$

TC(iii) $u \vDash B \wedge C$ iff $u \vDash B$ and $u \vDash C$,

TC(iv) $u \vDash B \vee C$ iff $u \vDash B$ or $u \vDash C$.

TC(v) $u \vDash B \supset C$ iff either (a) $u \vDash B$ and $u \vDash C$ or (b) $v \vDash C$ whenever $v \vDash B$ and $u \parallel v$.

We have the following derived clause for negation:

<u>Lemma 1</u>   In any model, $u \vDash \neg B$ iff not $v \vDash B$ for any v for which $u \parallel v$.

<u>Proof</u> $u \vDash \neg B = (B \supset \perp)$ iff either (a) $u \vDash B$ and $u \vDash \perp$ or (b) $v \vDash \perp$

whenever $v \vDash B$ and $u \parallel v$

iff never $v \vDash B$ whenever $v \vDash B$ and $u \parallel v$,

given that (a) cannot be satisfied and $v \vDash B$ would imply the truth of $\perp$ at v.

The logical notions of validity ($\vDash A$) and of consequence ($\Delta \vDash A$) and the like are defined in the usual way.

The following derived clauses are readily established and are stated without proof:

<u>Lemma 2</u> For any point u in any model $\boldsymbol{M}$:

(i) $u \vDash \top$

(ii) $u \vDash \bigwedge_{1 \leq i \leq n} A_i$ iff $u \vDash A_1, u \vDash A_2, \ldots,$ and $u \vDash A_n$

(iii) $u \vDash \bigvee_{1 \leq i \leq n} A_i$ iff $u \vDash A_1$ or $u \vDash A_2$ or ... or $u \vDash A_n$

(iv) $u \vDash \neg B$ iff not $v \nvDash B$ for any v for which $u \parallel v$

(v) $u \vDash \neg\neg B$ iff for any v for which $u \parallel v$ there is an w for which $v \parallel w$ and $w \vDash B$

(vi) $u \vDash B \equiv C$ iff either (a) $u \vDash B$ and $u \vDash C$ or (b) $v \vDash B$ iff $v \vDash C$ whenever $u \parallel v$

(vii) $\vDash B \supset C$ iff $B \vDash C$.

Models of Indeterminacy

We show how various indeterminacy claims are satisfiable. To this end, consider the model $\boldsymbol{M} = (U, \parallel, \varphi)$, for n $\geq$ 2, where

(i) $U = \{v_1, v_2, \ldots, v_n, w_1, w_2, \ldots, w_n\}$, for $v_1, v_2, \ldots, v_n, w_1, w_2, \ldots, w_n$ pairwise distinct;

(ii) $|| = \{<u, u'>: u, u' \in U \text{ and for no } i = 1, 2, \ldots, n \text{ is } \{u, u'\} = \{v_i, w_i\}\}$;

(iii) $\varphi(p_i) = \{v_i\}$ for $i = 1, 2, \ldots, n$ and $\varphi(p_i) = \varnothing$ for $i > n$.

(We might think of the $<v_i, w_i>$ as the husband-and-wife couples at a dinner party, where each spouse shakes hands with every other spouse though not with their own spouse). For the case $n = 2$, $\boldsymbol{M}$ has the following diagram:

$$
\begin{array}{cc}
v_1 & w_1 \\
p_2 \;\circ\!\!-\!\!-\!\!-\!\!-\!\!-\!\!\circ \\
\;\;\;\;\;\big| \;\;\;\;\;\; \big| \\
p_1 \;\circ\!\!-\!\!-\!\!-\!\!-\!\!-\!\!\circ \\
v_1 & w_2
\end{array}
$$

<u>Lemma 3</u> $I^*(p_1, p_2, \ldots, p_n)$ is true at any point in the model $\boldsymbol{M}$ above.

<u>Proof</u>   The following two facts are readily verified (where $1 \leq i, j \leq n$):

(i) $v_i \vDash p_i$ and $w_i \vDash \neg p_i$;

(ii) $v_i \nvDash \neg p_j$, $v_i \nvDash \neg\neg p_j$, $w_i \nvDash \neg p_j$ and $w_i \nvDash \neg\neg p_j$ for $i \neq j$.

Pf. (i) $v_i \vDash p_i$ since $\varphi(p_i) = \{v_i\}$; and $w_i \vDash \neg p_i$ since if $w_i || u$ then $u \neq v_i$ and so $u \nvDash p_i$.

(ii) $v_i \nvDash \neg p_j$ since $v_i || v_j$ and $v_j \vDash p_j$ by (i). $v_i \nvDash \neg\neg p_j$ since $v_i || w_j$ and $w_j \vDash \neg p_j$ by (i). The other two cases are similar.

It follows from (ii) that $v_i \vDash I^*(p_j, p_k)$ for each $1 \leq j < k \leq n$ (and similarly for w_i). For suppose $v_i || u$. Then u is of the form v_m or w_m. But $m \neq j$ or $m \neq k$. Suppose, without loss of generality, that $m \neq j$. Then by (ii), $u = \neg p_j$, $u \nvDash \neg\neg p_j$ and hence $u \nvDash (\neg p_j \vee \neg\neg p_j)$; from which it follows that $v_i \vDash I^*(p_j, p_k)$.

Since v_i (or w_i) $\vDash I^*(p_j, p_k)$ for each j and k, $1 \leq j < k \leq n$, it follows that v_i (or w_i) $\vDash I^*(p_1, p_2, \ldots, p_n)$.

Truth Tables

We show how to perform truth-table calculations within the present logic (though without presupposing that every statement is either true or false). These results are of some interest in themselves and are later critical in establishing the Possibility Theorem.

The following entailments reflect the calculation of truth-values. In each case, we show how the affirmation or denial of the components of a truth-functional compound is sufficient to determine whether it itself should be affirmed or denied.

Lemma 17 (Truth-functional Sufficiency)

    (i) $A, B \vDash A \wedge B$;

   (ii) $\neg A \vDash \neg(A \wedge B), \neg B \vDash \neg(A \wedge B)$

  (iii) $A \vDash A \vee B, B \vDash A \vee B$

  (iv) $\neg A, \neg B \vDash \neg(A \vee B)$

   (v) $A \vDash \neg\neg A$

  (vi) $A, B \vDash A \supset B$ and $\neg A \vDash A \supset B$

 (vii) $A, \neg B \vDash \neg(A \supset B)$.

<u>Proof</u> By a straightforward verification. For purposes of illustration, we consider the second part of (vi) and (vii).

(vi) Suppose that $u \vDash \neg A$. Then $v \not\vDash A$ for any v for which $u \| v$. So vacuously, $v \vDash B$ whenever $v \vDash A$ and $v \| u$; and so $u \vDash B \supset C$.

(vii) Suppose $u \vDash A$ and $u \vDash \neg B$. Then $v \not\vDash B$ for any v for which $v \| u$. Take any v for which $v \| u$. To show $v \not\vDash A \supset B$. Now not both $v \vDash A$ and $v \vDash B$, since $v \not\vDash B$. Also not ($w \vDash B$ whenever $w \vDash A$ and $w \| v$), since we have $u \| v$, with $u \vDash A$ and $u \not\vDash B$.

Let α be an assignment of truth-values (T or F) to sentence-letters. The assignment may be extended in the usual classical way to all formulas that are constructed from the sentence-letters on which α is defined by means of the connectives $\wedge$, $\vee$, $\neg$, and $\supset$. Suppose that α assigns a truth-value to each sentence letter of A and hence to A itself. Let A^α be the formula A if α assigns T to A and the formula $\neg$A if α assigns F to A; and let $SL^\alpha = \{p^\alpha$: p is the sentence-letter on which α is defined$\}$. The following result shows that there is a sense in which the connectives are truth-functional under the present semantics:

<u>Theorem 18 (Truth-functional Evaluation)</u> Let α be any truth-value assignment upon which the formula A is defined. Then $SL_\alpha \vDash A_\alpha$.
<u>Proof</u> By induction on the formula A using the results from the earlier lemma to cover the various cases.

We can use this result to establish a number of significant corollaries. We can show first that the system behaves classically under the assumption of LEM. Given a set of formulas Δ, let $LEM(\Delta) = \{p \vee \neg p$: p is a sentence-letter of a formula of $\Delta\}$.

<u>Corollary 19</u> Suppose A is a classical truth-functional consequence of the set of formulas Γ. Then $\Gamma, LEM(\Gamma \cup \{A\}) \vDash A$.
<u>Proof</u> Suppose A is a classical truth-functional consequence of Γ. By compactness, we can suppose that Γ is a finite set $\{B_1, B_2, \ldots, B_n\}$. Take any truth-value assignment α upon which A and $B_1, B_2, \ldots, B_n$ are all defined. There are two cases. (i) A is true under α. So by the theorem, $SL_\alpha \vDash A$ and hence $SL_{\alpha'} \Gamma \vDash A$. (ii) One of $B_1, B_2, \ldots, B_n$—say B_k—is false under α. By the theorem again, $SL_\alpha \vDash \neg B_k$; and so $SL_{\alpha'} \Gamma \vDash A$, as before. For each of the α upon which A and $B_1, B_2, \ldots, B_n$ are defined, let C_α be the conjunction of the members of SL_α and let D be the disjunction of the C_α. It is readily shown that $LEM(\Gamma \cup \{A\}) \vDash D$ and that $D, \Gamma \vDash A$; and so, by Cut, $\Gamma, LEM(\Gamma \cup \{A\}) \vDash A$.

Say that a formula is *unary* if it contains only one sentence-letter and that a unary formula is unary *in* p if p is its sole sentence letter. We use A(p) to indicate a formula unary in p. We then have the following important result on the compatibility of unary formulas $A(p)$ (which will be crucial in establishing the possibility theorem below):

<u>Corollary 20 (Compatibility)</u>   For unary $A(p)$:

(i) Either $p \vDash A(p)$ or $A(p) \vDash \neg p$; and, similarly, either $\neg p \vDash A(p)$ or $A(p) \vDash \neg\neg p$;

(ii) Given that $A(p)$ is satisfiable, it is compatible with p or compatible with $\neg p$;

<u>Proof</u>   (i) By theorem 18 (Truth-functional Evaluation), either $p \vDash A(p)$ or $p \vDash \neg A(p)$. If $p \vDash \neg A(p)$ then $\neg\neg A(p) \vDash \neg p$; $A(p) \vDash \neg\neg A(p)$ by (v) of Lemma 17; and so $A(p) \vDash \neg p$.

Similarly, either $\neg p \vDash A(p)$ or $\neg p \vDash \neg A(p)$ by theorem 18. If $\neg p \vDash \neg A(p)$ then $\neg\neg A(p) \vDash \neg\neg p$; $A(p) \vDash \neg\neg A(p)$ by (v) of Lemma 17; and so $A(p) \vDash \neg\neg p$.

(ii) By part (i), either $p \vDash A(p)$ or $A(p) \vDash \neg p$. In the first case, $A(p)$ is compatible with p since p is satisfiable. In the second case, $A(p)$ is compatible with $\neg p$ given that $A(p)$ is satisfiable.

The Possibility Theorem

We recall some definitions from appendix A, though adapted to the present linguistic framework. A *collective response* is a sequence $A_1(p), A_2(p), \ldots,$ $A_n(p)$ of formulas constructed from the single sentence letter p; and $A_1,$ $A_2, \ldots, A_n$ is said to be a *collective response to* $B_1, B_2, \ldots, B_n$ if $A_1, A_2, \ldots,$ A_n are respectively of the form $A_1(B_1), A_2(B_2), \ldots, A_n(B_n)$, where $A_1(p),$ $A_2(p), \ldots, A_n(p)$ is a collective response. A collective response $A_1, A_2, \ldots,$ A_n is *sharp* if

(i) $A_i \neq A_j$ for some $i, j \leq n$;

(ii) A_i is incompatible with A_j or $A_i = A_j$ for $1 \leq i < j \leq n$.

We similarly talk of a *sharp* response *to* $B_1, B_2, \ldots, B_n$.

We are now in a position to show that the present semantics is able to evade the impossibility result of chapter 1:

<u>Theorem 22 (Possibility)</u>   For $n \geq 2$, $I'[p_1, p_2, \ldots, p_{n+1}]$ is compatible with $\{p_1, \neg p_{n+1}\}$ and incompatible with every sharp response to $p_1, p_2, \ldots, p_{n+1}$.
<u>Proof</u>   We may show compatibility by reference to the model $\boldsymbol{M}$ above. Clearly, p_1 and $\neg p_{n+1}$ are true at v_1 in $\boldsymbol{M}$ and so, by the lemma 3, $I^*(p_1, p_2, \ldots, p_n)$ and hence $I^*(p_1, p_2, \ldots, p_{n+1})$ is also true at v_1.

Suppose now that $A_1(p_1), A_2(p_2), \ldots, A_{n+1}(p_{n+1})$ is a sharp response to $p_1, p_2, \ldots, p_{n+1}$. Then

(#) for each $i = 1, 2, \ldots, n+1$, $A_i(p) \vDash \neg p$ or $A_i(p) \vDash \neg\neg p$.

For suppose that this is not true for some i. By (I) of the above corollary, $p \vDash A_i(p)$ and $\neg p \vDash A_i(p)$. Now for some $j \neq i$, $A_j(p) \neq A_i(p)$ and $A_j(p)$ is incompatible with $A_i(p)$. Clearly we may suppose $A_j(p)$ is satisfiable, since otherwise it would be trivial that $I^*(p_1, p_2, \ldots, p_{n+1})$ is incompatible with $A_1(p_1), A_2(p_2), \ldots, A_{n+1}(p_{n+1})$. So by (ii) of the above corollary, $A_j(p)$ is compatible with either p or $\neg p$. Without loss of generality, suppose $A_j(p)$ is compatible with p. Since $p \vDash A_i(p)$, it follows that $A_i(p)$ is compatible with $A_j(p)$, contrary to the supposition that they are incompatible.

So $A_1(p_1), A_2(p_2), \ldots, A_{n+1}(p_{n+1}) \vDash \pi_1 p_1 \wedge \pi_2 p_2 \ldots \wedge \pi_{n+1} p_{n+1}$, where each π_k, for $k = 1, 2, \ldots, n+1$, can be chosen to be either $\neg$ or $\neg\neg$, depending upon whether $A_i(p) \vDash \neg p$ or $A_i(p) \vDash \neg\neg p$. But $\pi_1 p_1 \wedge \pi_2 p_2 \wedge \ldots \wedge \pi_{n+1} p_{n+1}$ and hence $\{A_1(p_1), A_2(p_2), \ldots, A_{n+1}(p_{n+1})\}$ is incompatible with $I^*(p_1, p_2, \ldots, p_{n+1})$.

REFERENCES

Black, M. [1937]. "Vagueness: An Exercise in Logical Analysis," *Philosophy of Science 4* (4), 427–55.

Field, H. [1994]. "Disquotational Truth and Factually Defective Discourse," *Philosophical Review 103*, 405–52.

Field, H. [2003]. "No Fact of the Matter," *Australasian Journal of Philosophy 81* (4), 457–80.

Fine, K. [1975, April–May]. "Vagueness, Truth and Logic," *Synthese 30*, 265–300; reprinted in Keefe & Smith [1997].

Fine, K. [2008]. "The Impossibility of Vagueness," *Philosophical Perspectives 22* (1), 111–16.

Fine, K. [2017]. "The Possibility of Vagueness," *Synthese 194* (10), 3699–725.

Gaifman, H. [2010]. "Vagueness, Tolerance and Contextual Logic," *Synthese 174*, 5–46.

Goguen, J. A. [1969]. "The Logic of Inexact Concepts," *Synthese 19*, 325–73.

Goldblatt, R. [1974]. "Semantic Analysis of Orthologic," *Journal of Philosophical Logic 3*, 19–35.

Graff-Fara, D. [2003]. "Gap Principles, Penumbral Consequence, and Infinitely Higher-Order Vagueness," in *Liars and Heaps*, ed. J. C. Beall and M. Glanzburg. New York: Oxford University Press, 195–222.

Greenough, P. [2003]. "Vagueness: A Minimal Theory," *Mind 112* (446), 235–81.

Greenough, P. [2005]. "Higher-Order Vagueness," *Proceedings of the Aristotelian Society, Supplementary Volume 79*, 167–90.

Goldblatt, R. I. [1974]. "Semantic Analysis of Orthologic," *Journal of Philosophical Logic 3* (1/2), 19–35.

Keefe, R., & Smith, P. (eds.) [1997]. *Vagueness: A Reader*. Cambridge, MA: MIT Press.

Keefe, R. [2000]. *Theories of Vagueness*. Cambridge: Cambridge University Press.

Kripke, S. [1963]. "Semantical Analysis of Intuitionistic Logic," in *Formal Systems and Recursive Functions*, ed. J. Crossley and M. Dummett. Dordrecht: North-Holland, 92–103.

McGee, V., & McLaughlin, B. [1995]. "Distinctions without a Difference," *Southern Journal of Philosophy 33*, Supplement, 203–51.

Parfit, D. [1971]. "Personal Identity," *Philosophical Review 80*, 3–27.

Peirce, C. S. [1902]. *The Collected Papers*. Cambridge, MA: Harvard University Press.

Sainsbury, R. M. [1989]. "What Is a Vague Object?," *Analysis 49*, 97–99.

Sainsbury, M. [1991]. "Is There Higher-Order Vagueness?," *Philosophical Quarterly 41* (163), 167–82.

Shapiro, S. [2005]. "Context, Conversation, and So-called 'Higher-Order Vagueness,'" *Proceedings of the Aristotelian Society, Supplementary Volume 79*, 147–65.

Smith, N. J. J. [2008]. *Vagueness and Degrees of Truth*. Oxford: Oxford University Press.

Sorensen, R. [2001]. *Vagueness and Contradiction*. Oxford: Oxford University Press.

Williamson, T. [1994]. *Vagueness*. London: Routledge.

Williamson, T. [2000]. *Knowledge and Its Limits*. Oxford: Oxford University Press.

Wright, C. [1975]. "On the Coherence of Vague Predicates," *Synthese 30*, 325–63.

Wright, C. [1987]. "Further Reflections on the Sorites Paradox," *Philosophical Topics 15*, 227–90; reprinted in Keefe & Smith [1997], 204–50.

Wright, C. [1992]. "Is Higher-Order Vagueness Coherent," *Analysis 52* (3), 129–23.

Wright, C. [2003]. "Vagueness: A Fifth Column Approach," in *Liars and Heaps: New Essays on Paradox*, ed. J. C. Beall and M. Glanzburg. Oxford: Oxford University Press, 84–105.

Zardini, E. [2011]. "Higher-Order Sorites Paradox," *Journal of Philosophical Logic 42*(1), 25–48.

INDEX

bivalence, 7–8, 13–14
   see also semantics classical, logic
      classical, excluded middle
Black, M., 24
borderline case, *see* indeterminacy local

classical, *see* semantics classical, logic
    classical
compatibility requirement, 18–21,
    23, 41, 43
  logic, 41
  model, 79
  relation, 41, 42, 45, 62, 79
  semantics, *see* semantics compatibility
  of a set of sentences, 74
  theorem, 84
commitment, 73
conjunctive syllogism, 47–49, 55
consistency, *see* inconsistency
cut-off, 13, 15, 20–21, 46–51, 55–56
cut rule, 73

D-closure, 72
degree of truth, *see* truth degrees of
degree theory, *see* truth degrees of
determinacy operator, *see* indeterminacy
distribution rule, 73

epistemicism, 8, 13–16, 17, 26, 40
elimination rules, 73
excluded middle, law of, 29, 32, 34, 35,
    41, 44, 45, 83
  see also classical logic
extremal premisses, 5, 46, 53

fact of the matter, 38, 38–40
  see also indeterminacy, truth
factuality, *see* fact of the matter
Field, H., 24, 38–40
Fine, K., xvi, xvii, 9n.1, 21n.2, 24
fission, *see* personal fission
forced march, 19–21, 23
  see also sorites

formula, 72
  unary, 83

Gaifman, H., 71
globalism, *see* indeterminacy global
Goguen, J.A., 9n.1
Goldblatt, R., 79
Graff-Fara, D., 71
Greenough, P., 24, 71

identity
  indeterminate, *see also* indeterminacy
    of identity
  personal, 45, 60–69
  rule, 73
  weak/strict, 64–65, 67–68
impossibility theorem, xvii, 21–22, 23–
  24, 40, 41, 43, 71–75, 85
incompatibility requirement, 18–21, 23,
  24, 41, 43
inconsistency, 74
indeterminacy, 2–3, 14, 40
  claim, 19–21, 23, 34, 42, 43, 45, 80
  global, xvi, 18–21, 24, 30–32,
    32–37, 40, 45
  of identity, 62, 68
  local, xvi, 10, 11, 14, 17, 18–21,
    24, 25–31, 34–37, 40, 45,
    51–52, 68-69
  models of, 80–81
  weak/strong, 35, 43, 68
intuitionistic logic, *see* logic
  intuitionistic
introduction rules, 73

Keefe, R., 9n.1
Kripke, S., 41
knowledge
  and determinacy, 28, 37–38
  safety, 37–38
  see also margin for error,
    transparency, epistemicism

law of excluded middle, *see*
  excluded middle
Lindenbaum, 75
localism, *see* indeterminacy local
logic
  classical, 7, 14, 29, 47, 54, 69, *see also*
    excluded middle, semantics classical
  compatibility, 40
  intuitionistic, 41
  quantum, 79
  of vagueness, 8
  see also modus ponens, sorites,
    semantics, truth degree of
luminosity thesis, 52–53, 55

margin for error, 53–56
McGee, V., 24, 27
McLaughlin, B., 24, 27
modus ponens, 5, 46, 49

Parfit, D., 64–69
Peirce, C.S., 25
penumbral connection, 10, 12–13
personal identity, *see* identity personal
  criterion of identity, 65–66
  fission, 60–69
  survival, 64–65
  well-being, 66–67
possibility theorem, 43–44, 82–86

quantum logic, *see* logic
Quine, 69

reductio, 73, 74
response
  bipartite, 77
  collective, 74, 76, 77, 84–85
  extremal, 75, 77
  individual, 74
  minimal, 19, 21, 23, 41
  sharp, 20–22, 23, 24, 41, 44, 75,
    77, 84–85

Sainsbury, R.M., 21
Sainsbury, M., 71
semantics,
    classical, 6–9, 11–12, 14
    compatibility, 42–43, 79–80
    see also truth degree of,
        supervaluationalism
Shapiro, S., 71
Smith, N.J., 9n.1
Sorenson, R., 9n.1
sorites argument, xvi, 2, 3–5, 8, 16,
        31–32, 45, 46–52, 56–60
    paradox, *see* sorites argument
    series, 7, 19, 32, 35–36, 42, 48
state description, 32–34, 40–41, 61–62
supervaluationism, xvi, 8, 11–13,
        17, 26, 41
survival, *see* personal survival

tolerance, 46–51, 53, 56, 57
transparency of mental states, 38,
        45, 52–60
transcendent illusion, 51–52

truth
    degree of, 8–10, 12, 16–17,
        26, 40
    determinate, 17, 20, 21, 26–27, *see also*
        indeterminacy
    of a formula, 42, 79–80
    non-deflationary, *see* determinate
    strong, *see* truth determinate
    tracking, 28–29
    see also bivalence

vagueness
    higher order, 20
    ordinary meaning, 1–2
    worldly, 3, 60–69
    see also indeterminacy

warranted suspense, 28–29
weakening rule, 73
Williamson, T., 9n.1, 25, 26, 52–60
Wright, C., 24, 46, 71

Zardini, E., 71